THE POWER AT WORK AMONG US

THE POWER AT WORK AMONG US

A Series of Lenten Meditations

by

D. T. Niles

LONDON

EPWORTH PRESS

First published 1968
by Epworth Press

Book Steward
Frank H. Cumbers

TO

DULCIE

*Printed in Great Britain at the St Ann's Press,
Park Road, Altrincham*

PREFACE

I have taken the opportunity given to me by the invitation to write a book of Lenten meditations, to plot an excursion through Scripture. The book itself is on the nature, I was about to say 'the structure', of the Christian life; but the method of the book is to go to Scripture and to listen to it. So to be able to read Scripture that the stories in the Old Testament become luminous, the teachings in the books of the prophets become contemporary and the writings of the New Testament become direct testimony to the presence and power of the Holy Spirit, is a continuing quest for every Christian. It is my prayer that in this quest, this little book too may be of help.

I have dedicated it to my wife whose companionship with me on this quest has been the richest of God's gifts in our life together. She has taught me much that otherwise I would have never learned.

D. T. NILES

FOREWORD

As one of the thousands who have benefited silently and anonymously from the previous writings of my friend, Dr D. T. Niles, I count it an honour to be permitted to raise my voice in commendation of this volume of Lenten meditations. Its title, as you will discover at once, speaks of the unconfined, abounding goodness, the grace and leading of God; but it is somehow descriptive of the book itself as well. The contents of these pages are far from being a collection of conventional passiontide devotions of the familiar type.

The day-by-day pilgrimage from Ash Wednesday to Easter Day on which you are about to set out is more varied than most earlier ones have been. It ranges, with a steady rhythm, from looking deep into the secret places of each one's own heart to summoning all of us to active, costly obedience in God's world outside. More insights dart and gleam on its pages. More of it quickens consciences. More unselfish resolves are aroused in the soul.

This is a testament of faith. There can be no mistaking that it has grown dynamically not only out of the author's intellect but out of his whole being. The faith to be found here is of the organic sort that comes from every part of human personality being lifted up to touch the whole of the One in whom we believe. Every chapter is marked with a sense of personal discovery and, in consequence, it can lead the reader to an equal discovery of his own. The man who enters into it with the right spirit will never find himself exclaiming: This or that would be good for a friend or acquaintance. He will say: This is wholesome food for me. Again and again a trenchant sentence will become a subject for meditation, for mastication, all day long.

The Power at Work Among Us is thoroughly scriptural. Although only a fraction of it is excerpted directly from the Passion story narrowly defined, it brims with the Gospel. All the essence of the good news in Christ—and its consequences for life—are in it. New Testament texts and Old Testament episodes are woven together in an arresting new pattern. The wine is in a new blend without losing a trace of its old distinctiveness or of its power to warm the heart of man. Light often shines from unexpected, often obscure, quarters of the Word, deepening appreciation in all of us for the richness and coherence of all that God has said. The man who wrote this book is steeped in the Scripture. I know no one who reads it with fresher eyes.

Another quality that I esteem in these meditations is the wholesome regard they exhibit for the Church. Nothing of the noxious and obnoxious attitude of disparagement of it that is so rife nowadays receives any aid or comfort here. Instead there is gratitude, a sense that God uses the Church to rear His children, a sound realization that Christian life is nourished in the Christian community. Much in this volume breathes the reverence that the Reformers used to feel for the mother of the faithful: nothing stoops to the disdain with which the Church is being brusquely dismissed by many today. This too is a whiff of healthy air.

The author, in case any of you do not know, is a scholar, pastor, educator, one-time staff member of the World Council of Churches, General Secretary of the East Asia Christian Conference, above all a liegeman of Jesus Christ. To him, and to his gracious and accomplished wife to whom he is dedicating this book, goes this salute.

Franklin Clark Fry

CONTENTS

'ONE THING I DO'

. . . because Christ Jesus has made me his own
. . . one thing I do . . . I press on (Phil. 3:13–14).

'Christ Jesus has made me his own.' There is no other beginning for the Christian life. We do not know when or how Jesus laid His hands on Paul, even Paul did not know. When, on the road to Damascus, Jesus confronted Paul, He told him that he was already yoked and that the cross-beam of the plough was already in its place, so that if Paul kicked, he would simply get hurt. Often we lay a too exclusive stress on our decision for Jesus Christ, forgetting that His decision about us is previous to ours and that our decision depends on His.

Paul never forgot the primacy of this action of Jesus on which everything depended. When he says, 'Jesus Christ has made me his own', he is giving expression to his ultimate certainty; that on which he rests, that by which he is sustained, that which determines everything that he must do. But these consequences in life which must follow Christ's action, never qualify that action. We remain His, both when we stand and when we fall. That is why He is both our Saviour and our Judge.

In his letter to the Romans, Paul says that the boundaries of his life are determined by the gospel. By it and for it, he is set apart (Rom. 1:1). He has no other interests. He seeks no other reward. He has but one concern. The gospel must be spread, and he must be used for its spreading. In his letter to the Philippians, Paul expresses himself differently. The emphasis this time falls not so much on the spread of the gospel as on the effect of the gospel

9

on Paul's own life. It has settled for him the direction his life must take. It has settled for him also his first priority. When he says, 'One thing I do', he means that that is the only thing which matters. 'I must press on, until I know as I am known, until I apprehend that for which I was apprehended, until I claim Him as my own who has claimed me as His own.'

The Lenten season is a time in the Christian calendar during which we seek explicitly to meditate on that action of God in Christ, by which we were found, and on the consequences in strenuous Christian living of that fact. Part of the problem that people have in understanding the Christian faith is that they seek to understand it as if it consisted of doctrines which they must believe and religious practices which they must keep. Doctrines and practices there are, but the essence of the Christian faith and life is that it is an activity. The New Testament speaks of it as a race to be run, a war to be waged, a wrestling to be undertaken. The whole business involves strenuous activity and vigorous discipline.

The only way to understand what it means to run a race is to train for it and to run it. The only way to know what it means to engage in a fight is actually to fight. The only way to know what wrestling is, is to meet one's opponent in a wrestling match. To be a Christian is to engage in an activity, recognizing that by such activity alone will understanding also come as to what the Christian faith is. How serious all this is finds expression in the words of Jesus, 'If your hand offends you, cut it off; if your eye offends you, pluck it out' (Mark 9:43f).

And yet we cannot leave the matter here, for as it is by Christ that we are launched on our course, it is by Him that we are also sustained. 'Your tackle hangs loose,' writes the prophet Isaiah (33:23); 'it cannot hold the mast firm in its place, or keep the sail spread out.' The wind will drive the ship but the sail must catch the wind. Only as the winds of God blow upon and into our faith will our lives find direction or drive. And when they do, how swiftly the ships go. But how may the mast be made firm so that the sail may be spread out? Only as it is placed in that one place where once a cross was raised. 'One thing I do'—that determination is valid : but before and beneath that determination is what He has done and is still doing, 'who by THE POWER AT WORK AMONG US is able to do immeasurably more than all we can ask or conceive' (Eph. 3 :20).

ASH WEDNESDAY TO SATURDAY

'Jesus Christ has got hold of me.' That is the thought with which these Lenten meditations begin. It seemed appropriate, therefore, to take for our first meditation the story of Palm Sunday, for at the centre of the Palm Sunday story is the ass which the Master wanted. Also, Palm Sunday speaks of the way in which Jesus comes, whether to the individual or to the world.

During the three days following Ash Wednesday, we shall meditate on the Apostles' Creed and its teaching concerning the basis on which the Christian faith rests. There are several ways of meditating on the Creed. What is attempted here is to see in the Creed the nature of the Christian hope. The Christian life is a life *en route*.

ASH WEDNESDAY

The Lord has need of it (Luke 19:31).

THE PREVIOUSNESS OF THE MASTER

'Go into the village opposite, where on entering you will find a colt tied; untie it and bring it here'. Just an ass, an ordinary ass, but the Lord is in need of it. The Christian life begins when one is found by God in Jesus Christ. It is the mercy and unexpectedness of this finding which the ass symbolizes. God found us, even though we were ordinary, very ordinary. Besides, how ordinary His ways were in finding us. God lays His hands through vision or surprising circumstances on only a very few. To most He comes in ordinary ways.

Lesslie Newbigin, at university, is preparing to go into his father's business, but is asked to give one year of service to the British Student Christian Movement before he goes. 'Help us for a year', that was all the request that was made. He agreed. And now he is a Bishop of the Church of South India. Just an ordinary request, but it was the way God's call came. Thomas Coke is pleading for volunteers to go with him to Asia. The first to offer his service is a young man with diseased lungs. The doctors had said that Squance had not much longer to live, but Squance was willing to go with Coke to Asia. Coke died on the voyage and Squance led that heroic band when they landed in Ceylon. For more than twenty years he pioneered the work of the Methodist Church in the North Ceylon District and opened Methodist work in South India also. Just an ass, an unlikely ass, but the Master wanted him and used him. Goliath is strutting before the Israelite army and King Saul is looking for somebody who will fit his armour. God finds a shepherd boy to challenge Philistine might. Goliath is defeated and God rides in triumph; but it is on an ass that He comes. Of all the villages of Palestine, Nazareth had the least reputation. 'Can any good come out of Nazareth?' they said. And yet when God became Man and walked this earth, He walked it as a Nazarene.

'When the Lord restored the fortunes of Zion
    we were like those who dream.
Then our mouth was filled with laughter
    and our tongue with shouts of joy;
then they said among the nations,
    "The Lord has done great things for them."
The Lord has done great things for us;
    we are glad' (Psalm 126:1-3).

The joy which this psalm expresses is the joy of a small

people who, in spite of their smallness, had received God's favour. The nations were surprised that the Lord had done great things for them, and they were surprised too.

The ass on which Jesus rode into Jerusalem was a colt on which no one had ever sat. A preacher was telling this story to some cowboys out west. At the end of the story, one of them is said to have remarked, 'What wonderful hands He must have had.' The preacher said to him, 'What do you mean?' To which he replied, 'Just think of an ass on which no one had ever sat and think of Jesus riding on it with men waving palm branches all around it and shouting for all they were worth. How difficult it must have been to manage that ass under those conditions. But Jesus did.' When Jesus waylaid Saul of Tarsus on the Damascus road, He was catching an ass whom man had never tamed. Jesus tamed him. The gay troubadour, St Francis, was an ass that only Jesus could have ridden. And only Jesus could have managed the volcanic independence of William Booth.

What is the Lenten season for except that, through its observance, we may be tamed and become the Master's ass. It has been said that men carry with them the history of their creation, and that even when they have managed to tame the lion and the tiger in them the donkey remains —a much more hardy animal. But the Lord can manage him, too. And, thank the Lord, He wants him.

Thinking about the way in which God found and tamed us, it is right also that we should remember how naturally the ass fits into the picture. The ass was part of his master's household. He stood before the platform of the one-roomed house of the *fellaheen*. It was his rightful place. In Botticelli's picture of the Nativity, the ass is shown looking at the baby Jesus, with Jesus laughing back at him. He had brought Mary all the way from

Galilee to Bethlehem, and now he stands looking in wonder at what he has done. The unexpectedness of his accomplishment takes him by surprise. No one has painted a picture of Jesus on the Mount of Olives weeping over Jerusalem, and painted into that picture the ass on which Jesus rode. We can imagine the ass standing there with the hands of Jesus upon him, supporting Jesus in His grief. The ass belongs to the Christian story. He gives to that story its homeliness. We are at home with Jesus because of the ass which is His companion, because of the ass on which He comes. There is no thunder and lightning, there is just the common round of sunrise and sunset. But as day succeeds day, Jesus comes nearer and nearer. How beautiful the meekness of His coming is. He finds an ass. How comforting the strength of His coming is. He tames the ass. How restful the naturalness of His coming is. He makes the ass His own.

G. K. Chesterton puts these words into the mouth of the ass:

> *The tattered outlaw of the earth*
> *Of ancient crooked will:*
> *Starve, scourge, deride me: I am dumb,*
> *I keep my secret still.*
>
> *Fools. For I also had my hour;*
> *One far fierce hour and sweet:*
> *There was a shout about my ears,*
> *And palms before my feet.*

The Christian faith is the announcement of God's triumphal entry into the world in Jesus Christ. He took human history and worked in it the divine event. He took human flesh and made it the divine tabernacle. He called ordinary men and sent them out as apostles to the nations. He chooses common folk to make increase of the

Body of Christ. The first Christian hymn is also the theme hymn of the Christian faith. The surprise in Mary's *Magnificat* is also our surprise, and its joy is our joy, too. So do we continue to hope in Him who has done great things for us—above all our deserving and above all our dreams.

THURSDAY

For in this hope we were saved (Rom. 8:24).

GROUNDS FOR HOPE

What is the basis of the Christian hope? In the last analysis, it is that God will accomplish what He has begun, and that the basic realities of life themselves tell us how trustable God is. When Paul says to the Gentiles that there was a time when they lived without hope, he couples with that also the fact that they lived without God (Eph. 2:12).

During these three days following Ash Wednesday, we shall look at the affirmations of the Apostles' Creed and see how these affirmations serve to strengthen us in the hope in which we were saved: for the Christian life, whose beginning is in being found of God, has to be sustained through a long day of strife and endeavour, until God himself has fulfilled His purpose in those whom He has found.

> *I believe in God the Father Almighty,*
> *Maker of heaven and earth.*

At the turn of this century, the world was in a mood of buoyant hope. Men felt that there was nothing they could not achieve with patience, with growing technical skill and with education. Today, the common mood is one of deep anxiety. Man is at the threshold of great possibilities and yet unsure of how to order life itself. Men have learned to distrust themselves. There is great activity but no hope.

To speak of hope at such a time demands a vision of possibilities that lie outside man. But, in order that it may not be wishful thinking, there must be the guarantee that the basis of such hope is trustable. The first affirmation of the Creed points to the hope that is implicit in the belief that this is God's world and that God made it: not simply that God caused the world, but that, since He made it, it remains His world—a world in which He will ultimately bring His purposes to pass.

I believe in Jesus Christ, His only Son our Lord,
Who was born of the Virgin Mary.

This world is more than a world which God has made. It is a world into which He came to live, as part of it. Many religions trace the suffering and sin of our world to human flesh. They conceive man's life as deriving its meaning from its attempt to obtain release from all that is mortal and changing. This kind of religion is a flight from life. What man needs is not a call to escape, but a call to overcome.

However, this can be attempted only if there is sure ground for hope that it can be achieved. Just here, the Christian faith makes its second grand affirmation. We know that this world is not evil, because Jesus is part of its history. We know that human flesh is not sin, because the Word became flesh. We know that time is not meaningless succession, because the life of the Son of God was lived in time.

*He suffered under Pontius Pilate, Was crucified
dead and buried; The third day He rose again
from the dead.*

The Word became flesh, therefore this world cannot be
denied; Jesus was crucified, therefore this world cannot
be affirmed. Hope must, therefore, lie in the possibility
of transformation, of redemption. Redemption is God's
promise to man, because Jesus rose again from the dead.
The writer to the Hebrews states the matter directly
when he says, 'As it is, we do not yet see everything in
subjection to man. But we see Jesus, crowned with glory
and honour' (Heb. 2:9). Our problem, however, is not
simply that we have a sense of frustration and hopeless-
ness, but that we suffer far more from a corroding sense
of drabness. Life becomes small and tends to be trivial.
The daily round and common task become a prison-house
of the spirit. But let a man come into personal relationship
with the living Christ and there breaks over his life a
splendour that is breath-taking. The power that raised
Jesus from the dead becomes active and available.

In this third affirmation of the Creed, a third truth
is affirmed about the world which goes beyond the two
truths that this is a world which God made and a world
into which He came. It is also a world in which the love of
God has been sown as a seed is sown, and which has died
as a seed must die, and which now bears fruit in the
power of a life that has been raised from the dead (John
12:24). The promise to make all things new is a promise
which is already being fulfilled. This is a world in which
the power of the resurrection is at work, a power which
keeps things fresh and makes them new (Rev. 21:5).

He ascended into heaven, And sitteth on the right hand of God the Father Almighty.

This fourth affirmation of the Creed is also an affirmation about the nature of the world. It says that this world and this universe are not a closed unit. They are governed by God and are open to His rule. This rule is the rule of Jesus Christ, which means that the cross and resurrection remain the methods of that rule.

In the world as we look around it, we see contending forces battling for the souls and bodies of men. While men in one part of the world are plagued by the problems of work, in another part of the world they are plagued by the problems of leisure. There are those who seek temporary relief in mass entertainment, alcohol, or drugs. There are others who seek permanent relief in a flight from life and sometimes even in suicide. For most it seems that there is nothing human goodwill can achieve apart from each person creating around himself an immediate circle of friendship. When the visible thus offers no ground for hope, is there an invisible reality on which hope can be based? There is. Men have 'a sure and steadfast anchor, a hope that enters into the inner shrine behind the curtain, where Jesus has gone' (Heb. 6 : 19). There is a throne above the universe and that throne is not empty. Hope does not arise from the circumstances of life, it arrives from the throne of God.

SATURDAY

He shall come to judge the quick and the dead.

The end of the journey is not when we arrive at journey's end; it is Jesus who arrives. He who started us out on the journey will himself come to meet us on the way.

This meeting with Him is the end towards which we go. In the book of Revelation, the New Jerusalem comes down from heaven, even though it has been a-building on earth. The completion of our obedience is by His action. On this action, the Christian hope finally rests.

The word in the New Testament which is used for describing this coming again of Jesus is the word *parousia*. This word has two related meanings. A *parousia* was the revealing of a presence always there, it was also the periodic visit of the emperor to any part of his far-flung domain. To say that Jesus is risen and to say that Jesus is ascended is to say that Jesus is here always as God. However, this presence of Jesus in the world which is discernible only to faith, becomes now and again a presence manifest to sight. It is like what happens when there is lightning. The sky is clouded and the night is dark, but, suddenly, there is a flash of lightning and everything stands revealed in its true proportions. When Jesus comes, it will be like that. And He will come like that again and again, until He comes finally both to judge and to redeem, both to end and to fulfil.

How then do we prepare to meet Jesus when He comes and whenever He comes?—by the life lived in the Holy Spirit within the fellowship of the Church. It is in the Church that Jesus is known already and confessed as Lord.

I believe in the Holy Ghost; The holy Catholic Church;

Thus, in this affirmation, too, there is being asserted a truth about our world—the truth that there is in it a community for whom the end has already begun and whose mission in the world is to be evidence and guarantee of the certainty of that end.

Amidst all other forms of human community, the

Christian community is intended to be the pattern of a people who know that this world is not their abiding place. Abraham is described as one who was looking for a city whose builder and maker is God (Heb. 11:10). Canaan becomes a symbol of man's true land of inheritance. But, in that it is an earthly symbol, it also signifies the truth that what is to be inherited finally in its fullness is already a present experience. As the writer to the Hebrews puts it, 'Faith is the title deed of things hoped for' (Heb. 11:1). The title deed has already been written. Present experience is the proof of that. And, because the title deed has been written, we know assuredly what we shall inherit.

The last sentences of the Creed tell us what that inheritance is, both in present experience and in future realization.

I believe in the Communion of Saints; the forgiveness of sins; The resurrection of the body, And the life everlasting.

THE FIRST WEEK IN LENT

Our meditation this week will be on the fact of faith. What are the contours of a faith which is scriptural? What light is thrown on this question by the very nature of the scriptural writings?

Also, what are the problems of faith? How is faith sustained and how is it tested? Using one episode in the story of Moses, we shall see how God offers to sustain faith; and then seek understanding of ways in which such faith is tested and through that testing is still maintained.

SUNDAY

Let the Word of Christ dwell in you richly (Col. 3:16).

OUR LIFE WITH HIM

There are those who are able to play by ear some piece of music which they have heard. However, no one who intends to become a musician can avoid learning music the disciplined way. When Paul says 'Let the Word of Christ dwell in you richly', he is asking that one should not only be able to read the musical score and play it, but that one should know the score. It must be in him. The Scriptures contain the musical score for the living of the Christian life. One way, therefore, of understanding the nature of that life is to understand it in terms of the kind of writings which the Scriptures are.

One of the commonest sayings among Christians is that the Bible has converting power. That is the conviction which underlies the work and strategy of all Bible Societies as they seek to disseminate the Scriptures to every people in its own language. But what is meant by saying that the Bible has converting power? Does it persuade those who read it about the truth of some body of teaching? We know that it is not that kind of book. It does not contain a persuasive and sustained argument driving to certain conclusions. Does it then set before those who read it, a way of life which appeals to them and which it constrains them to follow? It is not that kind of book either. It is not a book of high moral teaching which is set out in relevant relation to the problems of living. Does it commend itself as a book of praise and prayer and penitence on which the soul in its hunger for God can feed? We find that it is not even that kind of book—a religious book to meet the needs of religious man.

What kind of book then is it? And what do we mean when we say that it has converting power? In spite of over-simplification, the answer would still be right which is based on the fact that this book contains a record of preached events. It tells a story, and tells it in such a way that happening and meaning interpenetrate: so that as one reads it or listens to it, one sees, as it were, the inner texture of the drama of life itself and is drawn into the story as a participant. To become a participant—that is what it means to be converted by Scripture. The essence of what happens is not that one is persuaded of certain truths or is drawn to a certain manner of life or is helped and confirmed in one's religious devotions, but that one finds oneself accepting this story, as Scripture tells it, as including one's own story; and, therefore, acknowledging one's own place as participant within it.

The Scriptures have this effect because they are concrete in what they talk about. They do not, for instance, talk about what it means for something to happen but about the happenings themselves. They do not talk about man as they talk about men, nor do they talk about God in himself as they talk about God in what He does. The result is that he who reads finds himself challenged to accept his role as participant in this world and its history in the company of God whose activity and purposes make the human story both for individuals and for communities what it is.

An illuminating example of the nature of scriptural faith is the way in which, in Scripture, God is confessed. The very first sentence with which the Bible opens reads, 'In the beginning God created the heavens and the earth'. God is already known by the writer, and by the people to whom He belonged, as the God of their salvation: so that what is confessed is not only that God was their God, but that their God was God. Unless the God whom they had learned to confess from within their own history, was also Maker of heaven and earth, He could not be God. Indeed, it was because the God of Israel was God himself that Israel could not manipulate Him to her own purposes or fashion Him according to her own desires. That is why scriptural faith expresses itself not in terms of a discovery of God which men have made, but in terms of an acknowledgement of God into which men have been led. How inevitable it is that such an acknowledgement is introduced with a resounding 'nevertheless'. The nevertheless of faith affirms the existence of God and the love of God in the face of all the obvious evidence. This God, in His Love, faith confesses as purposive and as wielding sovereign power. He encompassed not only persons as persons, but persons in their relationships to one another, thus weaving and unweaving and weaving again the human community.

But, and here lies the realism of Scripture, this confession of God in relation to the world is made alongside an open-eyed recognition that the world can be organized and ordered outside Him. By using the word *cosmos* to denote this other world also, the New Testament is saying that here we are dealing with a viable alternative, with *cosmos* and not chaos, so that men can choose which world they really want. When the devil said to Jesus, 'These kingdoms are mine and I shall give them to you', he was not just boasting (Luke 4:6). There are two worlds and they are interlocked. How we shall choose between them, and how we shall live within them, is the ultimate decision towards which the Christian faith points.

How does Scripture convince men that they too belong to the story that is being told, and so challenge them to participation in it? Its first move is to declare that this is a world which God has made, which God loves, and which He has redeemed. There was a member of my church in Ceylon who lived a very difficult life. She became a widow very early, brought up her children under great hardship, lost two of them by death, and had the sorrow of seeing her eldest son come to live the useless life of a person addicted to liquor. I knew all that she had gone through. I went to visit her when she was in hospital, just before she died, and prayed with her. Because I knew her story, my prayer reflected it. I thanked God for His sustaining hand as He had made it known in her life. At the close of the prayer she took me by the hand and said, 'You forgot to thank God for all the mercies which He showed me which I never expected and for which I never asked.' I remembered the blessings she had not received, she remembered the surprises of God's goodness. The distinguishing mark of scriptural faith is that it asserts that these surprises tell us the truth about God and, therefore, about God's world. The Bible is not blind to the problems of life. It is deeply aware of the sins and sorrows with which life is furrowed. But it constantly bids us look behind and beyond, through the windows of surprise, so that we see life radiant with unexplained goodness. How appropriately are we told that the symbol of God's presence in the world is the rainbow! (Gen. 9:13; Rev. 4:3). The rainbow is proof that the sun is shining behind the clouds.

At this point, however, Scripture takes an unexpected turning. We would expect it to talk about the sun. Instead it talks only about the rainbow. The rainbow is all that one knows and can know about the sun. The rainbow is the product of sun and cloud. It is the perfect symbol of the father who sends the famine that brings the prodigal home (Luke 15:14), of the husband who takes his erring wife into the wilderness there to speak tenderly with her (Hos. 2:14), of the Lord who sends His people into exile but remains their sanctuary in the place where He has sent them (Ezek. 11:16), of the mother eagle who pushes her young ones out of the nest but carries them on her wings as they fall (Deut. 32:11).

One would have expected that if the story of man is thus determined by God's activity in salvation, then there would be an affirmation about men being saved from the world. But again Scripture faces us with the unexpected. It affirms the salvation of the world itself. The Incarnation event is the heart of this affirmation. God becomes part of that in which He was always involved.

The concern of God for the whole world and all its peoples can be seen on three levels. There is the fact that He is the Lord of every people. 'I who brought Israel from Egypt also brought the Syrians from Kir and the Philistines from Caphtor' (Amos 9:7). Secondly, there is set in the world a people of God who are the sign of God's rule and the token of His mercy. 'Arise and thresh, O daughter of Zion. You shall beat in pieces many

peoples and shall devote their gain to the Lord' (Micah
4:13). And thirdly, the rest of the world is itself the in-
strument of God's judgement and grace on Israel. Assyria is the rod of God's anger to punish Israel (Is. 10:5).
Cyrus is God's servant to set Israel free from captivity
(Is. 44:28). The warp of history is God's undistinguishing
regard for all, while the weft is the relationship of mutuality which He has established between His people and
His world. The end of the story, as the Bible depicts it,
is a city whose gates are always open, and only they are
left out who will not enter in (Rev. 21:25).

Against this background of the working out of God's
purposes, Scripture sets each man and all men. The truth
about God, it says, is also the truth about man; for God
and man belong together in the indissoluble connection
which is Emmanuel—God with us. Scriptural faith is
the explication of this 'with' in word and life and in its
full working out, this 'with' which is the source of all our
joys and all our sorrows.

MONDAY

Show me your ways (Ex. 33:13).

THE NEED TO KNOW

The story of the journey of the people of Israel from
Egypt to Canaan divides into two parts. The first part of
the story is the departing from Egypt. This phase comes to
its consummation at Mount Sinai. The second part of the
story is the journey to Canaan. In between these two
parts of the journey, there is recorded a conversation between God and Moses. What took place in this conversation makes a very good commentary on the require-

ments of faith. The conversation opens with Moses telling God of the situation in which he finds himself, now that he has been called to lead the people on this perilous journey. God has said to Moses, 'I know you, I want you, I have work for you.' And Moses has responded in obedience. The conversation between God and Moses takes place on the basis of this call and response. Indeed, it would have no meaning if not for the fact that Moses is already engaged to be the Lord's.

Moses begins by saying to God, 'You have given me this work to do. You have said that you know me by name and that I have found favour in your sight. Now, therefore, *show me your ways*. Tell me what the future holds.' He is aware that the journey from Mount Sinai to Canaan is going to be a difficult one. There will be uncharted sands to be crossed, marauders to be encountered, places where food and drink will be difficult to get, situations in which the people will lose hope and even lose their nerve. Moses wants to know what God is going to do in all these circumstances. God's answer is to say, '*I cannot show you my ways, but my presence will go with you* and I will give you rest.' In other words, 'I cannot give you any other assurance about the future, except that everywhere and under all circumstances, you will find me there. That alone must become for you the foundation of your peace. You must learn to find rest in the certainty that I am there and that I shall always be there.'

Moses had cause to know the full implication of this promise of God; for just before this conversation took place, there had happened the incident of the worship of the golden calf. If apostasy had not driven God away from His people, then nothing else would. God would indeed be there always, not only in every circumstance but in spite of every sin. The response of Moses to God is to say, 'If your presence will not go with me, do not carry us up from here.' One of the commonest mistakes that we make is to plan our own lives, to go where we want to go, and then somehow try to get God to be with us where we have gone. A friend of ours recently wrote to me and my wife asking us to arrange a marriage for her daughter. The letter ended with the words, 'Let whatever is God's will happen, but it must be a doctor.' Moses knows that there is no other way than to say, 'You take us where you want us to go.' That is the only true response to the promise of His presence.

But Moses goes even further than this. He says, 'How shall it be known that I have found favour in your sight, I and your people? Is it not in your going with us, so that we are distinct, I and your people from all other people that are upon the face of the earth?' The mark of faith lies not in our desire to ensure the presence of God with us, but in our willingness to keep company with Him on the way. The request of Moses was 'Show me your ways'. God's reply was simply to say 'I myself am the Way.'

TUESDAY

Show me your glory (Ex. 33 : 18).

THE NEED TO DISCERN

Moses makes a second request of God, '*Show me your glory.*' One of the difficulties which we always have, even though we know that God's presence is with us, is to discern that presence and to rest in it. If only God would reveal himself in His glory, if only His presence could be unmistakably radiant, how much easier it would be. This request of Moses should remind us of a later incident in the life of Elijah. At the moment of depression in Elijah's life, God came to meet His prophet. There was first a great and strong wind. But the Lord was not in the wind. Next, there was an earthquake, and then a fire. But the Lord was neither in earthquake nor fire. And after that, there was absolute quiet. Elijah heard the voice of God, as the voice of a gentle stillness (1 Kings 19:9). How often we have wished that God was in the wind or the earthquake or the fire! It would then be easy to discern Him. A baby's cry is heard in Bethlehem; that is the voice of God.

The answer of God to Moses was '*I cannot show you my glory, but I will teach you my goodness. I will make all my goodness pass before you.*' The clue to discern the presence of God in any situation is to remember how God has been with us in the past. We have known His goodness. Life is full of memories of God's guiding hand and overruling providence. We know how He has led us in ways we never dreamed of and filled our life with blessings for which we never asked. Moses could trace the goodness of God across the years. An Egyptian princess had saved him from death as an infant. A Midianite priest had ministered to him the counsels of God. He had lived in a palace and fled into the wilderness. He had been alone and now he was the leader of a people. He had spoken with God as a friend and now was pleading with God as a stranger. But throughout it all, he had learned one thing—that God was good. Now God says to him, 'Remember that goodness. I myself will evoke it in your memory and you will find that that is enough.' In the story of Jesus at the marriage of Cana in Galilee, the evangelist makes this comment : 'The steward of the feast did not know where the new wine had come from, but the servants knew' (John 2:9). They knew, because they had been involved in the making of that wine. Moses would be able to discern God's presence simply by being engaged in His service.

But the word of God to Moses goes even beyond this. He says, 'I will not only make all my goodness pass before you, but also I will proclaim before you my Name—"the Lord". I will be gracious to whom I will be gracious and will show mercy to whom I will show mercy.' There is no true knowledge of God's goodness which does not recognize the sovereignty of that goodness. There are those whose knowledge of God's goodness is not so much a knowledge of God who is good, as it is a knowledge about their own experience of His goodness. So they become self-conscious either of their faith in Him or even of their own goodness which they think has procured for them His favour. If Moses is truly to discern the presence of God, he must be aware how unmerited God's favour can be and how it overflows every barrier and boundary. Only then, can God's goodness provide the clue to the discerning of His presence.

WEDNESDAY

Show me your face (Ex 33:20).

THE NEED TO SEE

At this point in the conversation, God answers Moses' unspoken request. 'You cannot see my face,' He says, 'for man shall not see me and live.'

God knows us as we do not know ourselves. He knows us through and through. As the Psalmist says, 'He knows our thoughts before we think them. He knows us afar off. Such knowledge is too much for us. We cannot bear it

(Ps. 39 : 1–6). If God should look us in the face, we would die. So that when He says to Moses, 'I cannot show you my face,' it is because of His grace that He says it. But that is not the end of the matter, for Moses is vouchsafed another experience. God says to him, 'Behold, there is a place by me where you shall stand upon a rock; and while my glory passes by I will put you in a cleft of the rock, and I will cover you with my hand until I have passed by; then I will take away my hand, and you shall see my back; but my face shall not be seen' (Ex. 33 : 21–23). How true this picture is of God's ways with us. When He is most busy with us, He hides our face with His hand. It is not His face which He hides, but ours. It is we who must not see Him. He must see us, dealing with us in the ways in which we must be dealt with. But when it is all over, He takes His hand away and we see Him. We see as it were His back. We see Him in retrospect. We see Him in memory. And we know that it is He who has been with us all the time.

In this conversation between God and Moses, we are taught to see what the resources of faith are. *Moses wanted to know God's ways*; he was promised God's presence. It is essential to learn to live by that presence, to depend on it, to seek it, to be aware of it. Where this is done, whatever be life's story, it can be lived with God. *Moses wanted also to look on God's glory*; instead he was promised faith in God's goodness. It is very, very rarely that we can expect to have the experience of God's presence with us in its radiance. But always we can have God's presence with us in His grace. To remember this grace, to ponder it and allow life to be sweetened by it, is the way to keep faith hopeful and undimmed. *Moses wanted to see God's face*; he was told that he could have the assurance that it was God with whom he was dealing. What a precious thing this assurance is, for life is so full

32

of delusions and illusions, of shattered hopes and unrealized ambitions, of mirages and miasmas, that it is so easy to mistake shadow for substance and the false for the true. In its quaint way, the story talks about the experience of seeing God's back. But the point of the story is clear—God will see to it that we know that it is He with whom we are and in whom we live. Truly did John Greenleaf Whittier sing:

> Who fathoms the eternal thought?
> Who talks of scheme and plan?
> The Lord is God. He needeth not
> The poor device of man.
>
> Here in the maddening maze of things,
> When tossed by storm and flood,
> To one fixed ground my spirit clings;
> I know that God is good.
>
> I know not what the future hath
> Of marvel or surprise,
> Assured alone that life and death
> His mercy underlies.

THURSDAY

I would learn what he would answer me, and understand what he would say to me
(Job 23:5).

THE TEMPTATION TO UNDERSTAND

One of the constant problems of faith is that so much of the life of faith seems to have to be lived without understanding. It is all right to say God's ways are not our ways, and yet the problem remains as to how we can live with Him when His ways seem so incomprehensible. The book of Job is the most sustained attempt in Scripture to deal with this question. It chooses one aspect of the problem of life—the fact of pain and suffering—and discusses in terms of it, the ways of God with man.

There are two central themes in the book, and both can be expressed in the form of two questions which Job constantly asks of God: Show me my sin. Show me your reason. The first question is determined by Job's conviction about his own goodness, as well as his equal conviction that suffering is the result of sin. He is willing to accept that he would not suffer if not for his sin, but at the same time he has no consciousness of sin. He wants to repent, but he cannot repent of sins about which he does not know. If only God would show him his sin, the problem would be solved. The friends of Job attempt to speak to this need of Job. They want to help him to understand, but their answers are so much in terms of generalities that Job brushes them aside. What is God's answer to this cry of Job? The book of Job makes it clear that God does not accuse Job of sinning. He does not even allow Satan to do it. Indeed, the point which Satan wants to make with Job is that he has no sin and that, therefore, there is no point in serving God who will deal so harshly with one who has not sinned. Right to the very end of the story, the suffering which Job has endured remains unmerited suffering; and, therefore, Job's attempt to understand remains unfulfilled.

The second question which Job asks of God is: Show me your reason. This question arises out of the conviction which Job has that there must be some justification for what has happened to him in terms of God's good government of the universe. God's government of the world is an ordered government. There is always a reason for anything that God does. He is neither arbitrary nor capricious. Therefore, there must be a reason for all that

34

has happened to Job and his family. What God does with Job's request to understand is not even to say, 'Of course, there are reasons, but you do not have to know them'.

Instead, He asks Job the simplest and most direct of all questions, 'Have I to justify myself before you?' If God be God, it is He who has the right to ask questions and it is man who must answer.

If then, Job is not to understand, how is he to be satisfied? The answer given in the drama is that Job is finally satisfied with a vision of God which he receives. When Job sees God, he does understand what sinlessness is, so that he is driven to his knees in repentance. He is not repenting of his sins. What he does is to say, 'I despise myself' (Job 42 :6). Also, when Job sees God, he understands what God's wisdom is, so that he is led to trust that wisdom even though his questions still remain unanswered. There is no reply from God to Job's cry or questioning : and yet Job comes to see how to live with that silence. So must we.

FRIDAY

The Lord has prevented me from bearing children; go into my maid; it may be that I shall obtain children by her (Gen. 16 :2).

THE TEMPTATION TO BE HELPFUL

As the story has it, Abraham thought that the heir of his house would be his slave, Eliezer. But God said to him, 'This man shall not be your heir. Your own son shall be your heir.' Abraham believed God and waited. Many years passed, and yet there was no son. Then Sarah said to Abraham, 'It may be that what God meant was that you would have a son by my maid, Hagar.' (This was a perfectly proper understanding, because the son of the maid would legally be reckoned as the son of the mistress.) So Abraham took Hagar to himself and she conceived and bore him a son. Abraham called him Ishmael. Abraham was eighty-six years old at this time. When Ishmael was thirteen years old, Abraham has another encounter with God. God says to him, 'I am God almighty—the God who is sufficient in himself to fulfil His promises. The promise I made to you that you and Sarah will have a son will surely be fulfilled.' Abraham says to God, 'Sarah is already ninety years and I am a hundred. How can we have a child? Why not accept Ishmael as the child of promise?' But God says to Abraham, 'When I told you that you will have a son, it was not Ishmael whom I had in mind. However, I shall be with Ishmael also.'

We are told that it was after this conversation that the rite of circumcision was established. Abraham was circumcised and so was Ishmael, and every male among the men of Abraham's house. The appropriateness of putting the rite of circumcision, as having been adopted at this point in the story, is to point to the fact that Abraham was circumcised before Isaac was born. That is how Isaac is distinguished as the child of promise.

God's promise meant that Abraham and Sarah had to learn to live by it. Could the heir be Eliezer? Could he be Ishmael? We can see how Abraham tried to help forward the fulfilment of the promise by which he lived. But God's word to him was, 'Keep quiet and wait. I will fulfil what I have promised. I am able to fulfil what I have promised. I am God almighty.'

The next event in the story is when Sarah makes Abraham send Ishmael away. She says to Abraham, 'The son of this slave woman shall not be heir with my son, Isaac.' Yet Sarah's jealousy served God's purpose. Ishmael was sent away to become elsewhere the father of a great people, for God was with him, too. And Isaac grew up in Abraham's house to become Abraham's heir and the inheritor of the promises. However, here too, there is a turn in the story to notice; a turn provided by the demand which God made of Abraham that he sacrifice his son. Abraham had to learn the lesson that Isaac did not belong to him, but to God. Simply because Isaac was the child of promise, that did not mean that now Abraham himself was responsible to see that the promise reached its fulfilment.

The whole story is a complex one, but the thread of it is how God's purposes and promises were fulfilled in spite of human impotence, human mistakes and human sin. The problem of faith is to know when to wait and when to work, what to do and what not to do. It is also to know how to leave in God's hands the mistakes that one makes, so that not only is Isaac cared for, but Ishmael is cared for also. It is so easy to run before God in an attempt to help forward His purposes. It is also so easy to devise our own way of rectifying our mistakes, instead of allowing God to take care of them, too.

SATURDAY

Who is the God who will deliver you out of my hands? (Dan. 3:15).

THE TEMPTATION TO SECURITY

There is a story in the book of Daniel concerning three men, Shadrach, Meshach, and Abednego; and the way in which they were tempted to deny God. King Nebuchadnezzar had made an image of gold and commanded that all men should worship it. There is no suggestion in the story as to what or whom the image represented. It seems simply to have been the symbol of Nebuchadnezzar's own might and authority. Shadrach, Meshach, and Abednego were Jews who had been appointed over the affairs of one of the provinces of Babylon. But they would not worship the image which Nebuchadnezzar had set up. They were exiles in a foreign land, living by the favour of the king; but they were not prepared to accept the king as the final authority or arbiter of their lives. The king was furious when he heard about this and ordered the three men to be brought to him. He said to them, 'Is it true that you do not serve my gods or worship the golden image which I have set up? For, if it is, then you shall immediately be cast into a burning fiery furnace, and who is the god that will deliver you out of my hands?'

The answer of the three men is in four sentences—each a sentence of tremendous import: 'O Nebuchadnezzar, we have no need to answer you in this matter. If you do, as you say you will, our God whom we serve is able to deliver us; And He will deliver us out of your hand. But even if He does not, we will not serve your gods.'

We do not have to answer you. Shadrach, Meshach, and Abednego refuse to acknowledge that the king has any right to question them about the God they worship. Earthly authority has limits. It cannot claim to take the place of God or to regulate what men shall do in their worship of God. The three men who answered the king in this way are also declaring that, in the last analysis, they are not at the king's mercy. It is true that they live by the king's favour, but there is a point beyond which the king can neither do them good nor do them harm.

Our God is able to deliver us. So they make their next affirmation. They are in the hands of God, the God

38

they serve, who is powerful enough to deliver them from the king's hands. They assert this powerfulness of their God without any qualification. He can deliver us even from a burning fiery furnace. The faith of these three men is the faith of a people who had known their God through many a crisis and disaster.

Our God will deliver us. They not only assert that their God is able to deliver them, they assert also that He *will* deliver them. They have confidence that their prayer will be heard, that their faith will be honoured and that their hope will be realized. God will surely not let them down.

But even if He does not. And yet, having declared their faith in Him, they go on to say that they are prepared for God's non-intervention. One of the real problems for faith is that it is so natural to think that faith itself constitutes one's security. Shadrach, Meshach, and Abednego knew that they belonged to God and that even if God did not keep them safe from harm, they were still safe in Him. To be saved is to be safe whatever happens. This lesson has to be learned and learned well; for, in one way or another, the test will surely come when the choice is between choosing God and choosing a security which only God can provide. At such a time the temptation will always be to choose God if He will provide that security. Faith has to learn to say, 'But even if He does not, we shall still worship Him, and none other.'

SECOND WEEK IN LENT

The Christian life is a life we live together. It is a family life. The gathering together of this family is the burden of the New Testament story. It is not simply that the Christian life cannot be lived by each one by himself. It is rather that the Christian life must not be so lived. In the family are both the riches of and the disciplines for Christian living.

During this week, we shall look at the nature of this family life and the way in which it is nourished by God's gift in Jesus Christ. It is through Him that we have access to the Father and are also able to live with one another as children of one home.

SUNDAY

No one has ever seen God; the only Son, who is in the bosom of the Father, he has made him known (John 1:18).

OUR LIFE TOGETHER

We have already seen that Christian living is in response to an action of God, whereby men are known, are called, and are engaged in service. An equally important truth is that Christian life is life lived together. It is a people who are known and called and engaged to serve. In the conversation between God and Moses, Moses is quite conscious of the fact that he is not standing alone. He is the man to whom God has said, 'Bring up this people.'

He knows also that God's dealings with him as a person are bound to be conditioned by God's dealings with the people as a whole. In fact, when Moses makes his requests to God, he says also, 'Consider too that this nation is thy people.'

In the text which we are considering, the point is explicitly made that God can never be seen, and that He can only be known. God can never be object to our vision or to our knowledge. He is always subject who makes himself known by the ways in which He establishes relationships. We get to know Him by the ways in which He relates himself to us and the ways in which He relates us to one another. What is it that God has done, on the basis of which we are able to say, 'He has made himself known'? The evangelist says, 'Through Moses, God gave us the law; now, through Jesus Christ, he has given us himself.' The gift of law means that God has defined the limitations of man's freedom, determined the boundaries of his life and detailed the obligations which he must fulfil. Now, within this very life, so defined and delimited, He himself has entered as companion to man, leading man into an experience of the graciousness of truth. The law is also truth. But it is truth which is stern. In Jesus, truth was gracious.

To speak of the grace of God is to speak of the graciousness of God. However, there is a misunderstanding to be guarded against. God is never gracious in the sense that He is indulgent. My eldest son said to me one day, 'Whenever I am troubled or angered or in doubt, I have to test myself against you. It is against you that I can hurl my emotions or my ideas. If I cannot do this with you, then with whom can I do it?' He would not have adopted this attitude to me if I had been an indulgent father. For, in that case, there would have been no limitation against which he could have pulled himself up.

When parents are indulgent, they create a sense of insecurity in their children. The child left to its own devices, without the protection of the 'Yes' or 'No' of its parents, has to look after itself. It is too young to do this. The result is that it becomes inhibited and afraid. God is gracious, but He is also truth.

The evangelist says that this revelation of God as gracious truth came through the Son. In a later passage in the gospel we read, 'No man comes to the Father but by me' (John 14:6). Jesus is the way to the Father, because He is the Son of the Father. He represents what it means to be the Father's son. 'To those who accepted him,' the evangelist says, 'he gave authority to become the children of God' (John 1:12). Why is such authority or permission necessary? Because the prodigal cannot just walk into his father's house. He has to be forgiven, and the forgiveness has to be authoritatively declared. It is not enough that sins are forgiven in the sense that the guilt is taken away or that the consequences of sin are cancelled. Forgiveness means, fundamentally, restoration to the Father and to the life of the whole family. This is why the experience of forgiveness in Jesus Christ has its peculiar connotation. It is more than a transaction between God and the sinner. The flock is a scattered flock, until every lost sheep is found. The chain cannot be worn until all the ten coins are hanging on it. One lost coin means a useless chain. The prodigal son has to be restored not only to the father, but also to the home. The father's forgiveness of the boy who has come back has serious consequences and imposes obligations on the brother who never went away (Luke 15:3–32). When John says, therefore, 'No man has ever seen God; the only Son, who is in the bosom of the Father, he has made him known,' he is pointing to the nature of the life together which is involved in Christian living.

There is a second text in the first epistle of John which also begins with the words, 'No man has ever seen God.' But the second part of the text is different: 'If we love one another, God abides in us and his love is perfected in us' (1 John 4:12). The relation between these two texts is clear. Jesus makes God known by loving us. We make God known by loving one another. The verse in John's epistle which gives us the connection between these two texts reads as follows: 'In this is love, not that we loved God, but that He loved us and sent His Son to be the expiation for our sins' (1 John 4:10). The expiation for sin which John is talking about is an expiation for the sins of all mankind. There is only one act of forgiveness and it includes all men. This is man's indivisible heritage, so that we either enjoy it together or not at all. To find forgiveness is to participate in the forgiving activity of God. To be an object of His love is to become the subject through whom that love flows out to others. To be loved and to love are indivisible parts of one experience. God is revealed by Jesus who loved us and by us in whose lives His love flows out in loving relationships.

In the teachings of Jesus, this emphasis on love, not simply as an obligation to be fulfilled but as the only means by which God's love for oneself can be known and experienced, finds constant repetition. In the passage in Matthew's gospel, to take one instance, where Jesus is talking about our relation with our fellows, the whole argument depends on the one word 'brother'. The other man is brother already, because God is Father, and the way in which I treat my brother decides also the way in which I treat my Father. That is why it is right that I should be judged by the way in which I treat my brother (Matt. 5:21f). In the Genesis story, Cain asks the question, 'Am I my brother's keeper?' God's judgement of Cain is based on the fact that Cain has to account

43

for Abel, because Abel also belongs to God. My brother is my brother, because he is God's son, and every Abel is God's accepted son (Gen. 4:9).

All this means that it is impossible to understand the nature of the Christian life, except as it is understood in terms of the family relationship, as well as in terms of God's purpose to make himself known. These two always belong together. The Christian life carries with it the connotation that it makes God known. It points to what God is like and, because this is so, it can never become a purely individual affair. It has to be life within the family. By the family is meant both the family which is constituted by response to God's action and the family which is constituted by the action itself. The latter is the human family, for all are children of the one Father. The former is the family in Christ and is made up of those who have accepted the consequences and obligations of having been loved by the Father through the Son. The family life lived by the Christian family must issue in strengthening and sweetening the family life of the human family.

Often, the statement is made that the consequence of the fatherhood of God is the brotherhood of man. That is not so. The consequence of the fatherhood of God is the family of man. I have four brothers and four sisters. When our father was alive we were a family, when he died we were still brothers and sisters. But we had ceased to be a family. However, neither the Christian family nor the human family can thus be dissolved : for the God who is our Father is established for us in the fact of a risen Christ. The family relation remains an eternal relation ; so that brotherhood becomes not an obligation to be fulfilled, but a gift of the resurrection to be received. So is the Christian life sustained by the promise, 'because I live, you shall live also' (John 14:19).

44

Blessed be the God and Father of our Lord Jesus Christ (Eph. 1 : 3–14).

OUR INHERITANCE

There is someone whom we can call ours. We can call Him ours because God gave Him to us. 'God so loved . . . that He gave His . . . Son' (John 3 : 16). He is ours also, because He was not ashamed to call us brethren (Heb. 2 : 11). His Father is our Father. His God is our God. 'I go', He said, 'unto my Father and to your Father, my God and your God' (John 20 : 17). God's new name is now, as the New Testament has it, 'God the Father of our Lord Jesus Christ.' When we speak about our inheritance, it is about Him that we speak—Jesus Christ. Everything else we inherit, we inherit in Him and because of Him.

'Consider what God has done,' says Paul, and then lists seven things that God has done to us and for us in Jesus Christ.

(1) He chose us.
(2) He destined us to be His sons.
(3) He redeemed us, freely forgiving our trespasses.
(4) He made grace abound to us in all wisdom.
(5) He gave us insight into the mystery of His will.
(6) He sealed us as His own.
(7) He gave us the Holy Spirit as the guarantee of our inheritance.

When the text tells us that God chose us before the foundation of the world, it is emphasizing the fact that what has happened to us is not the result of some whim of God, but is according to His eternal counsel. It is something on which we can depend. The import of this choice is that we should be His holy and blameless children,

45

'living within His constant care'. So we learn to praise His glorious generosity, remembering that we have received His welcome into our share of the love He bears to His beloved Son. This welcome means that forgiveness has been wrought for us. The forgiveness of our sins is a deed done on which we can take our stand. Nor has it been done hesitantly or half-heartedly. Indeed, what has been done has been done so lavishly that it has caused an overflow into our lives, opening our eyes to the truth. The life of each one of us has, as it were, become a speech about Jesus Christ. It is well to ask ourselves : What does my life say about Jesus Christ? What does it sound like when it is looked upon as a speech about Him? Nothing less than this is involved in bringing our lives under the heading which is Christ.

What then is it that has essentially happened? We have become His inheritance and He has become ours. The Holy Spirit with whom we have been stamped is the guarantee of our purchase, 'until the day when God completes the redemption of what He has paid for'. The experience of the Holy Spirit is also the first instalment of what we ourselves shall inherit; for we shall inherit God himself and our place in the fullness of His work which He has now begun in us and in His whole creation.

TUESDAY

He destined us to be his sons through Jesus Christ (Eph. 1 : 1–13).

OUR HOME

This same passage that we have looked at, in trying to understand the nature of the Christian inheritance, furnishes us also with a description of the home in which the

Christian life has to be lived. The Christian life is a life lived together by those who belong to Christ in the Church which is their common home. The Church is the result of the call of God. It is the society where the healing processes of Christ are at work. It is the habitation of the Holy Spirit, God at work in the world.

When we speak of the Church as the result of the call of God, we need to remember that this call is from time immemorial. In the garden of Eden itself God's voice is heard saying, 'Adam, where are you?' (Gen. 3:9). The same wail of God is heard in the words of Jesus, 'O Jerusalem, Jerusalem, how often I would, and you would not' (Matt. 23:37). When Paul says, 'We have been called', he is speaking of the way in which we have been made the people who will take to all the world the message of God's concern for them.

In the references to the Church as the society where the healing processes of Christ are at work, the emphasis is on three facts—here God's word is proclaimed; here His means of grace are administered; here the fellowship of His family is realized. As the epistle has it, 'Christ is the head of the Church being himself its Saviour, the Saviour of the body which is his bride. For, he loved the Church and gave himself for it, that he might cleanse it and sanctify it and present it to himself a glorious Church, holy and without blemish' (Eph. 5:22–27). The Church can never be understood in static terms. It is always in the process of becoming. It is the Church, because Christ is at work in it, perfecting it according to His own purposes. To be in the Church is to be exposed to this working of Christ. Whenever His word is proclaimed, His saving action becomes contemporary. He who gave himself for the Church, gives himself to His people again and again as they receive in the Church the means of grace. He who is perfecting His Church, perfects it in fellowship,

47

for in the fellowship of the family of God is the true experience of the fellowship between God and His people.

At Bethlehem, human flesh became the habitation of God. In the upper room, human community became God's habitation. Pentecost is the culmination of God's method in the redemption of history. When we speak of the gift of the Holy Spirit, we are speaking not only of the experience of God as He indwells the Church and every member of it, we are also speaking of the consequence for the total human community of the presence of the Christian community within it. Jesus said to His disciples, 'Wait for the Holy Spirit, for when he has come, you shall receive power to be my witnesses' (Acts 1:8). This power, at work through the Church in the world, is what we are talking about when we are talking about the work of the Holy Spirit. Jesus said of Him, 'When he comes, he will convince the world of sin and of righteousness and of judgment' (John 16:8).

WEDNESDAY

I love thee, O Lord, my strength (Ps. 18:1).

OUR PILGRIMAGE

In the Epistle to the Hebrews, we read that God was not ashamed to be called their God because they acknowledged that they were strangers and exiles on the earth (Heb. 11:13–16). The people of God never settle down. They keep going till they arrive at home. Peter, in his first letter, greets those to whom he writes 'as aliens and exiles' (1 Pet. 2:11). He warns them against those who would constantly be seeking to make them settle down. They will oppose you, he says, and be against you because

48

God is their disturber. You must so live in their midst that they may see God as their salvation.

In the eighteenth psalm is a full description of the situation and experience of the pilgrim. The first three verses celebrate God who is the inheritance of the pilgrim. 'I love thee, O Lord,' is how the psalm begins. It is that love which sustains the pilgrim throughout his way. In the next three verses, the psalmist calls upon the Lord to deliver him from all his perils. 'God heard my voice,' he says, 'and my cry to him reached his ears'. Here we have expressed the primary relation on which man's pilgrimage depends—God who is the pilgrim's love and attraction, as well as his companion on the way.

Verses seven to eighteen describe the deliverance which God effects for His servant. God comes down, incognito but effective. He knows that the perils with which the pilgrim has to contend are too big for his unaided strength. In verse nineteen is a simple statement of the nature of the experience of salvation which God brings. 'He brought me forth into a large place because he delighted in me.' What God does, He does because He loves. Why He delights in me, I do not know. But that He does, I can see. Verses twenty to twenty-four contain the kind of statement which occurs again and again in the Old Testament. The psalmist is unable to grasp the full implications of what he has already said. He feels that he must give a reason why God delights in him. This passage is a very good example of the temptation to which God's children are prone, the temptation to think of themselves as in some way distinguished.

Verses twenty-five to twenty-seven do not quite escape the way of thinking which is found in verses twenty to twenty-four. But in these verses we have the transition which those who are God's children must always make— the transition from themselves to others. I must constantly remember that God deals with others as He deals with me, and that He deals with me as He deals with others. The psalm goes on from here to express the confidence of the psalmist as he faces the future. God will do for him whatever needs to be done. 'Thou dost light my lamp; Yea, by thee I can crush a troop; and by my God, I can leap over a wall. Thou didst give a wide place for my steps under me, and my feet did not slip.'

Verses thirty-seven to forty-five give a description of a battle. Indeed, this psalm is not a psalm of pilgrimage. Its choice to illustrate the pilgrim's life has been made, because the moods through which it passes do illustrate that life. The battle that is described is a battle of a man with his enemy. It is immaterial for our purpose that this is so, for the point is that the pilgrim has a battle to wage which is no less serious. The psalm ends on a note of confidence—'The Lord lives'. The pilgrim's daily existence is in the awareness of this livingness of God. God is the pilgrim's love and desire, his sustenance and his deliverance, the goal of all his endeavour and the hope of his daily trek.

THURSDAY

For where your treasure is, there will your heart be also (Matt. 6:21).

OUR TREASURE

There are four contrasts which are worked out in the course of this sixth chapter in Matthew's gospel. The first contrast is that between God and man. Jesus is speaking of the practices of piety: alms-giving, prayer, and fasting. The point he makes is that, since these are the accepted practices of piety, those who observe them get the reputation of being pious people. The result is that the practices are often undertaken in order to win this reputation. The warning of Jesus is that men should not expect a reward from God in addition to the reward from man. Where the praise of man is desired and obtained, the whole transaction is then over. There is nothing left for God to do. The thrust of this teaching is that piety is fundamentally a question of one's relation to God. When the right relation is maintained and one receives an earthly reward also, he who receives it knows whether it is from God or from man; or when one does not receive an earthly reward, one knows whether it is God who refused it or man who prevented it. The constant problem is to see that piety remains a way of experiencing God and does not deteriorate into a way of experiencing piety.

The second contrast is a contrast between heaven and earth. The question at issue is where or on what one's heart is set. If the heart is set on earth, then even the practices of piety can become means of increasing one's treasure on earth. When this happens, when earth takes the place of heaven in one's desires, light becomes darkness. It is not possible to serve God and mammon, for mammon is all absorbing even as God is. So that the love of mammon can turn the very things which are intended to bring to us the experiences of heaven into instruments for bringing to us the experiences of earth.

The third contrast is between what we receive and what we acquire. Food and clothing and shelter are God's gifts and can be so received. But men become so anxious about these, that they set out to provide these for themselves. They lose sight of the fact that food, clothing and shelter are part of God's provision for men together and that, therefore, the way to obtain them is to seek the kingdom of God and the doing of His will among men. When I seek my own food, or food for my family, I am

51

engaged in one kind of operation. When I seek to improve the economy of my country and its food production, then I am engaged on another kind of operation. Care for all must take the place of anxiety for oneself.

The fourth contrast is between today and tomorrow. God provides us with sufficient strength and sufficient grace for the tasks and troubles of each day. We run out of strength and become graceless and tense by attempting to crowd into today the problems which belong to tomorrow. God's provision is day by day, even though His promises abide for ever. Because we trust these promises, we must learn to live one day at a time—learn to let the day's own trouble be sufficient for the day.

FRIDAY

I am under obligation . . . so I am eager to preach the gospel to you also (Rom. 1 : 15).

OUR SITUATION

The situation in which the Christian stands is well expressed by Paul in the simple phrase, 'I am under obligation.' The Christian life is life in the gospel, but this gospel is never one's own. It has to be proclaimed if it is to be believed in. Indeed, there is no way of living by the gospel except by sharing it with others. Not only must the good news be told, but we must recognize also that the good news is news about others and, therefore, must be told to them. Paul says, too, that he longs to see the Christians in Rome, so that he may impart to them some spiritual gift, that thereby he and they may be mutually encouraged. This is the other side of the situation in which the gospel places us. In a true conversation about the gospel, we not only tell the good news but also

52

listen to it. Indeed, even when we are talking to those who are not Christians, if we listen carefully, we shall find that they, too, are telling us about the ways in which God in Christ has been at work in their lives. News of the Christ-incognito is also good news. Too often, we are so anxious to tell the good news that we miss listening to it.

But why does Paul conclude with the words, 'I am not ashamed of the gospel.'? It is because he wants to say that it is no shame to be a man under obligation. It is no shame to live by something which also belongs to everybody else. It is no shame to be known as a purveyor of news, when that news is news about the power of God for salvation to everyone who has faith. It is common experience that men seek distinction by comparing themselves to their fellows and claiming that they possess what others do not possess. There is the distinction of rank and position, of wealth and learning, of caste and class. To be just one of the common folk looks like a disgrace. For Paul, it is no disgrace that the gospel has defined him as a man like everybody else, whether they be Jews or Gentiles. In the gospel, all men are equal and all are equally men. This situation, says Paul, in which the Christian life has got to be lived enjoins, on each Christian and on the Christian community as a whole, an obligation which must be discharged.

First of all, the gospel becomes gospel, only when it is proclaimed. In fact, part of the good news is that God constantly calls and commissions those who will proclaim it. Besides, he who proclaims is himself part of the evidence of the event that is being declared. In another place, Paul speaks of the aroma of the Christian life (2 Cor. 2 : 15). That is a good metaphor for describing the nature of the Christian witness. Nor may we forget that the perfume of true holiness can travel against the wind.

The task of identification is essential to the task of proclamation. We cannot speak to our fellowmen with the astonished contempt which the elder brother showed when his younger brother came back home. We need so to become part of those to whom we speak that our words will carry for them the compulsion of their own inner voice. To identify is not a method of evangelism, it is the logic of the incarnation. However, we must remember this, that becoming part of the gospel and part of its evidence can happen only at the frontier; that is, where the gospel meets the world in all its needs. He who is proclaiming the good news must be so identified with his hearers that the gospel meets him in meeting them. He must stand at the point of explosion.

And finally, the obligation to share the gospel must be discharged by declaring it not only to men but also to communities. There must be the attempt to change individuals as well as to change the structures of society. It was a world which God loved; that is, men and women in the totality and complexity of their relationships. He who said, 'Behold, I send you as sheep among wolves' (Luke 10:3), is the good shepherd of the sheep and of the wolves.

SATURDAY

And you shall know that I am the Lord
(Ezek. 11:10).

OUR GOD

When the prophet emphasizes the importance of knowing God as Lord, he is emphasizing the fact that apart from the recognition of this Lordship, there is no clue to life's meaning. The twists and turns of the life we have to live together can only be understood as we recognize that this life is always lived under God and that He remains within it the Lord who decides.

The story, in this chapter of Ezekiel, opens with twenty-five men sitting at the gateway to the temple. Among them are Jaazaniah, the son of Azzur, and Pelatiah, the son of Benaiah, princes of the people. These men are identified as men who give wicked counsel in the city. The prophet delivers to them the word of God, telling them that God's punishment will fall on them. 'I will judge you at the border of Israel; and you shall know that I am the Lord, for you have not walked in my statutes nor executed my ordinances, but have acted according to the ordinances of the nations that are round about you.' Even as the prophet is prophesying, God's judgement falls. Pelatiah dies. Whereupon the prophet falls down upon his face, crying to God and saying, 'Lord God, wilt thou make a full end of Israel?' The reaction of the prophet is not to rejoice at the vindication of his prophecy, but to sorrow for the people against whom he has prophesied. He knows his God. He knows that when punishment comes, it will be more than a pure vindication that God is God. Punishment is never the end.

God's answer to the cry of the prophet is to say, 'Whereas I have removed them far off among the nations and whereas I have scattered them among the countries, yet will I be to them a sanctuary for a little while in the countries where they are come and they shall know that I am the Lord.' The God who has punished is also the God who affords sanctuary. How naturally a child, punished by its mother, still wants to cry enfolded in its mother's arms. Paul gives expression to this same truth about God when he says, 'No temptation has overtaken you that is not common to man. God is faithful and he will not let you be tempted beyond your strength, but with the temptation will also provide the way of escape, that you may be able to endure it' (1 Cor. 10 : 13). We are never at the mercy of the testing we undergo. We go to pieces under our punishment only when we refuse to accept God as our sanctuary. It is then that we become hard and brittle, and break.

But God's answer goes even beyond saying that He will be their sanctuary in the land of exile. He will do more than that. 'I will give them,' He says, 'a new heart and put a new spirit within them. I will take the stony heart out of their flesh and give them a heart of flesh, that they may walk in my statutes. And they shall be my people and I will be their God.' *I will punish you, I will be a sanctuary to you, I will restore you*—it is I who do these things and these things which I do will teach you that I am the Lord. Also, when obedience springs out of forgiveness, the tension is gone. But—and this 'but' always remains—those who do not change, who still insist on exploiting God's forgiveness, who refuse to accept that God is Lord—to them God says, 'I will requite their deeds on their own heads.'

'Hell is for the blind and not for them that see', so that if we insist on being blind we must end up in hell.

THE THIRD WEEK IN LENT

A consideration of the family nature of the Christian life must lead us to the fact that this life is not merely lived in the world, but bears a saving relationship to the world. The Christian family is within the human family. The story from the life of Paul which is used to illustrate the mutuality of this saving relationship between the Church and the world is a part of the story of his journey to Rome.

The six meditations which follow work out this same theme. They are based on six stories in the Old Testament in which the emphasis is on the nature and consequences of the relationship between those within the family of faith and those who are without.

Sunday

God has granted you all those who sail with you
(Acts 27:24).

OUR LIFE IN THE WORLD

Among the stories of Paul which we have in the Acts of the Apostles, one story has always impressed me as holding within itself a parable. Paul was being taken as a prisoner to Rome. This voyage was proving to be hazardous, because it was already winter. The story says that when they were in Fair Havens, Paul advised the centurion not to proceed with the voyage. He said, 'I perceive that the voyage will be with injury and much loss, not only of the cargo and the ship, but also of our lives.' But the centurion did not listen to Paul. He paid more attention to the captain and the owner of the ship. Also, most of the passengers wanted to proceed with the voyage, because Fair Havens would not at all be comfortable in the winter. They wanted to reach Phoenix, a more suitable harbour in Crete, if possible.

Here we have the opening theme. Those in charge of the affairs of the world see no reason why they should listen to the counsels of the Church. How often the prophets of the Old Testament were in this situation! Statecraft demanded an alliance with Egypt, but the prophet advised against it. National honour demanded rebellion, but the prophet counselled submission. War demanded stern measures, but the prophet pleaded for mercy. Military weakness demanded compromise, but the prophet advocated resistance. Is it any wonder that, so persistently, the word of the prophet was not heeded? In our own time, how equally persistently are we told that the Church must keep out of politics! It is one thing, the men of the world say, for the Church to enunciate general principles, it is another thing for the Church to speak specifically with respect to any situation.

According to the story, the centurion not only preferred to listen to the captain and owner of the ship, but he listened also to the passengers whose one idea was to get out of the discomfort of their situation. Phoenix would be a more comfortable place to winter in. And, as the story has it, a south wind blew gently, raising false hopes. This was unexpected, though exactly what was wanted; so that they took the risk. But the risk did not pay off. There is nothing more dangerous than wishful thinking. Soon the ship was caught in the midst of a lashing storm. The cargo had to be thrown overboard; and even the tackle of the ship had to be discarded.

At this stage appears the second theme of the story. Paul gathers all his fellow-passengers together to announce to them their true hope. He says to them, 'I had a dream. I was told that I would accomplish this voyage in safety, for God has decided that I shall bear witness to Him before Caesar. And God has granted me all of you who are sailing with me.' As far as the ship owners were concerned, the ship was going on an ordinary trading voyage. But, the determining fact in the story of the voyage was that it was carrying a missionary. Paul is being taken to Rome to preach the gospel there. That decides what will happen to Paul and to Paul's companions. When we say that the Jesus-event is the midpoint of history, we are saying also that His message and its messengers remain the out-thrust of this event and carry its significance.

The third theme in the story comes at the point when the sailors, discovering that the ship was nearing some rocks, seek to escape in the lifeboat under the pretence of lowering anchors. Paul intervened and said to the centurion, 'Unless these men stay in the ship, you cannot be saved.' This particular phase of the story is a suggestive one. Faced by danger, there was the tendency for each to seek his own security. The whole enterprise looked like disintegrating. It was Paul who held the ship together. Here is a role which the Church has to play again and again. How much has depended, and how much still depends, on the little communities of Christians among the new nations of Asia and Africa, to preserve these nations from the fissiparous tendencies of group selfishness! And how big has been the price which was paid when the Church in any land failed the nation at this point!

Before we come to the climax of the story, there is a sub-theme which is worth noticing. Because of the danger they were in, those on the ship had undertaken a fast. They had gone without food for fourteen days. Paul encouraged them to eat. They were already safe because of God's promise. But, even if this were not true, nothing was gained by fasting. The religious temptation, somehow to bring pressure upon God to aid man in his extremity, has to be resisted. There is a form of religion which is the very antithesis of living by the good news.

The climax of the story was when the ship ran aground and the passengers were able to swim ashore. The soldiers, afraid that some of the prisoners might swim to freedom, wanted to kill them. But the centurion, wishing to save Paul, kept them from carrying out their purpose. This is a touching part of the story. Every aspect of the missionary enterprise shows evidence of how, again and again, it has been served by the kindness of men and women in all walks of life and in all kinds of positions of authority. Also, in the story itself, how literally the promise was fulfilled that Paul's fellow-prisoners were saved because of him!

Is it just fancy to read this story of Paul in this way? I do not think so. The fact is that there is a connection between the Church and the world and that, because of the nature of this connection, it is possible to use such a story as this to illustrate it; not that the story itself proves anything, but that, when it is seen as a parable, it is so seen only because the gospel-event itself gives us the perspective for looking at it in this way.

The gospel-event is a secular event. It belongs to the world. That is why the climactic command which is laid upon the Church is, 'Go and tell.' The gospel-event is something which can be proclaimed because of the secular nature of its happening. There are those who say, 'Yes, a child was born, a man lived and died. And all

60

this happened for any man to see. But how is it that the Church includes in its proclamation the resurrection and ascension of Christ? Surely, only they who had faith saw the risen Christ or spoke of His ascension?' This protest, voiced by so many, must be well taken; but the reply to it lies in a deeper analysis of what is meant by the secular. Was not the command 'Go and tell', in the first place, a command concerning the resurrection-event itself?

We live in an ordered world. The relation of this world to its Creator is part of its texture. It is dependent on Him. So that, when we speak of the Jesus-event as a secular event, we are saying that something happened in the world and to the world—that this event belongs to the very texture of secular reality. Thus, the death of Jesus on the cross is a secular event, not only in the sense that a man died on a cross for all men to see, but that it is a secular event also in the sense that by His death something happened within the relation of the world to God, a relation which is itself part of secular reality. The resurrection of Christ, too, is a secular event in this sense. When Christ rose from the dead, an event of explosive significance took place within the relation between God and the world. Faith discerns the significance of that death on the cross. Also, it is to faith that the risen Christ presents himself. But both event and meaning belong to the secular. They are part of the texture of secular reality.

In meditating on the story of Paul's voyage to Rome, we commented on the significance of the fact that Paul was going to Rome as a missionary even though he was going as a prisoner. That is the determining factor in the story. The missionary movement continues the secular significance of the gospel-event. It is part of the inner structure of history. When Abraham was called by God, God said to him, 'I will bless you and in you the nations

61

of the earth will bless themselves.' The heritage of Abraham was other people. In the story of Jacob and Esau, we see acted out the nature of the choice which man must make in relation to God's purpose in the world (Gen. 25:29–34). When Esau returned home from his hunt he found Jacob eating pottage. He asked Jacob for that pottage because he was hungry. Jacob said, 'You must choose—choose between your heritage and pottage.' Esau chose to give up his heritage. What was the use of other people anyway? He would rather live and make sure of the means of living. This is always the basic choice: either the world for myself or myself for other people: and it is possible to be religious whichever the choice be that is made.

In the picture by Holman Hunt entitled 'The Light of the World', Jesus is standing outside a closed door knocking. He is asking the person who is inside to come out and go with Him on His mission. But the man inside has shut the door against the world. It is not improbable that there was a chapel inside that house where he worshipped regularly. In the story of the man from Gadara, who was cured by Jesus of his madness, the man asked Jesus whether he could go with Him. He wanted to live the religious life. Jesus asked him to go back to his home and to his village and to all the secular responsibilities which he had so long left unfulfilled (Luke 8:39).

The Church is turned towards the world, that is its chance. The command to it is to 'go into all the world' and there to preach, baptize and teach the nations—that is, men in all the particularities of their social existence. At the last Conference of the European Churches, Dr Visser 'tHooft declared, 'Our task is to confront European culture with those basic questions which it must face, if it is to have a future. Our evangelism should not be a church-centric evangelism. It should raise the issues of European existence and raise them in the light of of the Christian gospel. We would perhaps call it a Socratic evangelism in which the evangelist is midwife rather than preacher.' In other words, we are faced with the responsibility of being the Church in relation to all those who sail with us.

But with the command to go into all the world is also given the promise, 'I am with you'. He is with us because He goes before us. He is there wherever we go before we get there. The angel message is always literally true, 'He is risen and goes before you into Galilee' (Matt. 28:7). He is with us also not only because He goes before us, but because it is He who takes us. It is never true that we take Him. He is the giver, we are the gifts—gifts of His love for those to whom He sends us.

What does He do with us as He sets us facing the world? What does He do with those whose companions we are on the way? Let us look at some concrete examples in order to find an answer. In the Old Testament, we have the long and circuitous story of the people of Israel. But while that story is told from the point of view of God's relations with Israel, the story itself is set within a larger story—that of the rise and fall of the ancient kingdoms of Philistia and Phoenicia, Egypt and Syria, Assyria and Babylon, Persia and Greece. The movement of Israel is a part of the movement of the nations. God used the nations to carry Israel towards its destiny.

In modern times, too, a similar story can be written concerning the relation of the modern missionary enterprise to the rise and fall of modern empires. From the days in which the missionary moved along the Roman roads up till today, the Christian missionary has been carried where the ships have gone taking the administrators of empires to their posts or the builders of trade to their markets. Every missionary journey is a part of an ordinary journey—an ordinary part of ordinary life. However—and this is where the mystery lies—God, who uses the movements of secular life to carry the missionary and his message to the peoples, also commits them into the missionary's hands.

The first truth remains, then, that it is the world which administers the gospel to the Church. The world is the means of calling a church to its obedience as well as of chastising it in its disobedience. When a church has to carry the cross, that cross is fashioned for it by the world. When a church is to be as a city set on a hill, it is by the world that the situation is contrived. It is within the movements of world history that the missionary movement is set, it is through the pressures of that history that the Church discerns its times and seasons. But even as the world administers the gospel to the Church, so the Church declares the gospel to the world and makes that gospel effective in the lives of men. For that which is promised to the Church is for the world also. The promise of God to Paul included Paul's companions also.

In the Division of Inter-Church Aid and Refugee World Service of the World Council of Churches, it is an accepted principle that human need is met and alleviated simply as human need. This is right. But, when the Church adopts such an attitude, it does so precisely because it is the Church, and because to it, as evangelist and missionary, have been granted all those who are its companions on the way. Men are served simply as men; but he who serves, serves as evangelist. Indeed, it is precisely because both service and witness are functions of the missionary as missionary, that they have each their own validity.

There is still a further sense in which we must take note of the interlocking of the Church and the world—a sense which is not suggested in the story of Paul, on which we are meditating, but which we must take seriously into account. It is the sense suggested again and again in Holy Scripture, when one reads the words, 'I have delivered your enemy into your hands' (1 Sam. 24:4). It is in this situation that the Church and every Christian face the ultimate demand that the enemy, who is at one's mercy, has to be forgiven. Forgiveness is the consequence of God's forgiving mercy towards all men, so that to forgive is to participate in this forgiving activity of God. The specific assertion of the Christian faith is not that men do not know the experience of forgiveness outside Jesus Christ, but that only in Jesus Christ is this experience of forgiveness turned towards the world. To know that one is forgiven by Jesus Christ is to find oneself involved in the forgiving activity of Christ in the world. The psalmist asks God to keep his path straight because of his enemies. When others wrong us, the temptation to retaliate is such that we allow our own actions to become crooked. We let the enemy decide how we shall behave, instead of behaving according to our own nature as the forgiven children of God.

It is a serious responsibility when men, whether enemy or friend, stranger or neighbour, in want or in wealth, in distress or despair, are committed into our hands. But the situation itself is an inescapable one. To be bound to the secular is to be bound to other people. To serve the Lord is to serve those for whom He died. To be engaged in His mission is to be engaged to all those who are our companions on the way.

Then the Lord said to Cain, Where is Abel your brother?
(Gen. 4 : 9).

CAIN AND ABEL

In the third chapter of Genesis, we have the first question
which God addresses to man, 'Where are you?' In the
fourth chapter, we have His second question addressed
to man, 'Where is your brother?' Cain answers, 'I do
not know.' But God replies, 'You must know, for I can
hear the voice of your brother's blood, and it tells me
that you have done something to him. What have you
done?' Cain's plea is that he is not his brother's keeper.
Why should he be held responsible for looking after
Abel? Abel should be able to look after himself. This
world is a world of keen competition, a world in which
each man should be allowed to drive the hardest bargain
that he can. Consideration for other people is bound to
be misconstrued as weakness. Cain was simply saying,
'If Abel could not protect himself, that is not my
fault.'

The answer which Cain receives is a revealing one.
God says to him, 'The earth has opened its mouth to
receive your brother's blood from your hands. It is by
this earth that you too must live. So that, when you till
the earth and seek to live of its fruit, it will return to you
the fruit of your brother's blood also. You cannot escape
this. Wherever you go it will be so.'

God has bound men, each to other, in such a way that
the whole of life is knit together into one whole. A man
can destroy his brother but he cannot get rid of him. The
brother he destroyed remains part of life, part of the very
life which the destroyer must live. What a good modern

example we have of this, in that nations wage war against one another and then find that the nation which wins becomes responsible for the ongoing life of the nation that loses! Or, in the world of commerce, how essential it has become for the nations which make the profits to give away part of their profits in aid to those from whom the profits were made, in order to prevent the whole process of commerce itself from breaking down.

Brother sheds the blood of brother, but the blood that is shed remains part of the life which has to be lived. No wonder Cain cries out and says, 'My punishment is greater than I can bear.' It is at this point that the story takes a sudden turn, for even though Cain has refused to accept responsibility for Abel, God cannot refuse to accept responsibility for Cain. Cain cannot be treated by others as Cain treated Abel, for God will inquire what happened to Cain just as He inquired concerning what happened to Abel. So the Lord puts a mark on Cain.

The story concludes with the sentence which defines the nature of human life as it has to be lived in tragedy, though not in despair. 'Then Cain went away from the presence of the Lord.' He still wears the mark that God has put upon him, the mark which means that he will carry with him always his experience of God's presence, the presence in which he was established in responsibility to his brother and in which others were established in responsibility to him. And yet, he goes away from God's presence, for henceforth the felt absence of that presence is going to be for him the determining fact in his life.

*Then the Lord said to Noah . . . and Noah did all
that the Lord had commanded him* (Gen. 7 : 1–5).

NOAH AND THE NATIONS

God begins again. That is the message of the story of
Noah. The story begins with the statement, 'The Lord
saw that the wickedness of man was great in the earth,
but Noah found favour in the eyes of the Lord.' The
reason that is given for God's favour towards Noah is
that he was a righteous man. However, there is nothing
in the story itself which gives substance to this character-
ization of Noah, except that he believed God and did as
God commanded him to do. Also, there is nothing
special said about the members of the family of Noah.
They were just like everybody else who was destroyed.
This is the kind of biblical story in which the question
as to what actually happened is quite immaterial. The
point to be emphasized is simply and directly made, and
is not allowed to rest on the credibility of the story itself.
The emphasis here is not so much on the fact that everything and everybody else was destroyed, as on the fact
that Noah and his family were saved. There is never any
getting away from the overtaking judgement of God, and
yet never does this judgement issue in a destruction so
complete that there is no possibility of a new
beginning.

When the floods had abated and Noah and his family
came out of the ark, God said to Noah and to his sons
with him, 'Behold, I establish my covenant with you and
your descendants after you and with every living creature
that never again shall all flesh be cut off by the waters
of a flood.' The purpose of Noah's story thus becomes
clear. It is to show that human history is the result of the

patience and mercy of God. Because He will not destroy, therefore He must redeem. The rainbow is the sign that the rains will cease and that the sun will shine again. God's wrath is always present, but God's mercy is what men live by.

It is not possible to deal with the story of Noah without also dealing with the story of Babel (Gen 11:1–9). The two stories belong together and determine for us the perspective in which to see human history. In the story of Babel, men are shown to be unbelieving of God's covenant not to destroy. They seek, therefore, to build their own security. They want to build a tower that goes up to heaven, so that if it should rain again as it did in the days of Noah, they can go up that tower to heaven itself. God will not then be able to destroy them without destroying himself. This attempt on the part of man to create security for himself by involving God in his own predicament is a constant preoccupation in every religion. The more men are able to bind themselves and God together, the more secure they feel; but God will not allow it. Men must learn to believe in a God who is not just part of themselves.

In this story of Noah and the story of Babel, we have as it were the backdrop to human history—a backdrop in which the point is made that there is no distinction between man and man in terms of race or religion or morality. God's covenant is with all men, and man's doubt of that covenant, as sufficient basis for life, is a doubt in each man's heart. The story of Babel ends with the picture of men unable to understand one another and to work together. It is a true picture. Men build true community only as that community is dedicated to live by and to serve God's will and purpose. No true community can be built in the service of wrong. Human selfishness makes that impossible.

*The Lord said, Shall I hide from Abraham what
I am about to do?* (Gen. 18:17).

ABRAHAM AND LOT

Right in the middle of the story of Abraham is this episode concerning Lot. Lot was Abraham's nephew and
came with Abraham to the land of Canaan. As the story
has it, the call of God was to Abraham and Sarah and
their descendants after them. But when Abraham left
his country to go to the land of promise he took Lot with
him, and Lot remains in the story the symbol of those
who belong and yet do not belong to the people of God
in the world.

When Abraham arrived in Canaan, it was Lot who
was given the first choice of the part of the land he would
occupy and chose the most fertile part. The cities which
grew up in that part of the land were Sodom and Gomorrah. They were so rich that they became the envy of
others. The next episode in the life of Lot was when he
was taken captive by the kings who came to war with
the kings of Sodom and Gomorrah in order to capture
these rich cities. Abraham went out to war on behalf of
Lot and rescued him.

Now comes the third episode in Lot's life, when God
decides to destroy Sodom and Gomorrah because of the
wickedness in them. Abraham, to whom God has revealed His intention, pleads with God for the two cities,
'Wilt thou indeed destroy the righteous with the wicked?
Suppose there are fifty righteous within the city, wilt
thou then destroy the place and not spare it, for the fifty
righteous who are in it?' Abraham's intercession is per-
sistent until God finally assures him, that even if there

be ten righteous in those two cities, He will not destroy them.

There is hope for Sodom and Gomorrah, if there are at least ten people in them who will be witnesses to God's righteousness. Of course, if God spares the cities on this account, all those who are spared will not know what lies behind the impunity with which they are able to live their wicked lives. They are bound to think either that there is no God or that, even if there is, somehow God can be bribed or manipulated. There must have been many temples in Sodom and Gomorrah where this attempt to bribe and manipulate God was highly organized. And yet, God is willing to commit His cause into the hands of ten people. However, it turns out that there are not these ten. Even Lot's sons-in-law do not count. Lot's very wife could not be counted. So the cities are destroyed and only Lot is saved and his two daughters. The story makes plain that these two daughters, too, should not have been counted. They were simply rescued with Lot. A meaningful part of the story is in the incident in which Lot asks permission not to flee to the hills, but to go to one of the suburbs of the cities that were being destroyed. God grants him this request so that, even in the destruction of Sodom and Gomorrah, there was a remnant which was saved.

As we can see, the story of Lot contains many themes which intertwine and show how closely knit is the relation between the people of God who bear His name and those who do not. Lot accompanies Abraham and inherits the richest part of the promised land. Abraham goes to war on behalf of Lot. Abraham intercedes before God on behalf of Sodom and Gomorrah. Not only does Lot escape, but his daughters also. And finally, even the destruction of the two cities is not a complete destruction.

This story, too, ends in a way which underlines another

71

tragic aspect of human life. Lot becomes the father of the peoples of Ammon and Moab, peoples who remained, through the early part of the Old Testament story, the enemies of the descendants of Abraham.

THURSDAY

Then the word of the Lord came to Elijah, Arise go to Zarephath (1 Kings 17 : 8).

ELIJAH AND THE WIDOW

In the first sermon of Jesus as recorded in Luke's gospel there are two incidents from the Old Testament to which He refers (Luke 4 : 16f). The first of these is the incident of Elijah being sent to Zarephath in the land of Sidon to a woman who was a widow. In the way in which Jesus quotes the incident, the emphasis falls on the blessing which the woman of Zarephath received from God through Elijah. But, as the story is told in the first book of Kings, it was the woman of Zarephath through whom, in the first instance, God looked after Elijah.

When Elijah asked this woman for a drink of water, he was already asking for something that was scarce. But when, on seeing how promptly she responded to his request, he asked her also for a morsel of bread, he was really putting her to the test. There were many adequate reasons which the woman could have given for not being able to look after Elijah. She could have said, 'You are a Jew, I am a Gentile. You are a man, I am a woman. Besides I am a widow and I am poor. Kindly, therefore, go somewhere else.' Instead of this, while she told Elijah what her actual condition was, she nevertheless gave him what he wanted. The result was that she found herself provided for throughout the whole period of the famine. The jar of meal and the cruse of oil did not fail.

How often it is true that it is when we have good reasons for saying 'No' that we have to say 'Yes'. In God's ways with men, the unexpected is so often God's way, that we have to learn both to expect the unexpected and to welcome it. The point that Jesus makes is that amidst the famine, God made special provision for a Gentile woman who was not even an important person. She was just a peasant woman, a poor widow. Indeed, the woman receives far more than she gave. She gave Elijah food and the God of Elijah gave her food in return. But God also gave her back her dead son. When her son died, she felt that in some way Elijah was responsible for the calamity. Then she discovered to her surprise that Elijah was responsible for her deliverance from that calamity.

In this story of Elijah and the widow of Zarephath, we have a perfect example of the way in which God's grace in salvation operates. If we use Elijah and the woman as symbols of the Church and the world, we can see how God's saving action comes to the Church from the world and to the world from the Church. The story ends with the words of the woman to Elijah, 'Now I know that you are a man of God.' When she first accepted him, she did not know. She simply had accepted him as fellowman.

This is the saving relationship in which men are bound to one another. As in Jesus' parable of the last judgement, they who ministered to the hungry and the thirsty, the prisoner and the stranger, discovered in the end that it was by these very people that Christ had been mediated to them. The story of Elijah and the widow of Zarephath is an Old Testament episode illustrating this same truth. God had prepared that woman in Zarephath to look after Elijah. 'Behold, I have commanded a widow there to feed you,' is how the text reads. But in arranging for her to feed Elijah, God was also arranging for Elijah to feed her. Not only were Elijah's needs being met, but also her prayers were being answered.

FRIDAY

Elisha the man of God sent to the king, saying,
Let Naaman come now to me (2 Kings 5:8).

ELISHA AND NAAMAN

The story of Naaman is the other incident that Jesus refers to in His sermon at Nazareth. It is a story with many twists and turns. The first fact in the story is that the person responsible for bringing the news of the availability of God's grace for curing Naaman is a little slave girl. She has been brought from the land of Israel as the result of a raid on Israel by Syria. She is part of the spoil of battle. The word of God comes to the master through the servant, to the conqueror through the conquered, to him who keeps the prison through him who is in prison. The second episode in the story is when Naaman arrives with a letter to the King of Israel from the King of Syria. The King of Syria believes that the King of Israel has the means of curing Naaman. The King of Israel, however, not only does not know that he has the means but thinks that the King of Syria is simply seeking a quarrel with him. Why was not the King of Israel as aware of Elisha, the man of God, as was the slave girl in the home of Naaman?

In the third episode in the story, Naaman is angry that he has not been treated with the deference due to him. It was a difficult lesson for Naaman to learn that,

74

in Elisha's eyes, he was only a leper. His status as a commander of the Syrian army meant nothing to Elisha or to Elisha's God. Men always find this fact a great difficulty. They think that worldly position and wealth can somehow mitigate the fact of their leprosy. Naaman came with his horses and chariots and halted at the door of Elisha's house. And Elisha sent a messenger to him saying, 'Go and wash in the Jordan seven times.' Naaman was not only angry that Elisha did not come out to meet him, he was also disappointed that Elisha did not cure him directly. 'I expected him,' he says, 'to call on the name of the Lord his God. Instead of which he wants me to go and wash in the river Jordan.'

Why must Elisha choose this way? He chooses it because that is God's way. It is God's way so to mediate His grace that men must bend to receive it. The significant and the ordinary become invested with insignificance, with the result that there is no extraneous aid to faith. There is nothing about the river Jordan to persuade Naaman that it is worth washing in it. When at last he consents to go to the river Jordan and wash, he does so simply and only because that is the command he has received. It is worth noting that it was Naaman's servants who finally persuaded him to do the humble thing. They were used to doing menial tasks. They say to Naaman, 'If the prophet commanded you to do some great thing, would you not have done it? How much rather then when he says to you, wash and be clean.'

The last two episodes in the story are each the reverse of the other. When Naaman is cured, he decides to serve the God of Elisha. He asks from Elisha two mules' burden of earth which he can take back to Syria, so that on it he can build a temple to Yahweh. He also expresses repentance in advance for his attendance at the temple of Rimmon to which he will have to go accompanying his king. That was part of his official duty. But whereas Naaman turns to the Lord, Gehazi, the servant of Elisha, turns away from Him. When Naaman offered Elisha gifts of gratitude for his cure, Elisha refused to accept them. If Naaman himself did not belong to God, he could not satisfy the situation by simply giving gifts. Gehazi on his part, however, wants to exploit the situation for his own benefit. The result is that he is struck down with Naaman's disease. Here is stern warning that the gospel may not be exploited for worldly gain. Whenever and wherever that is done, those who do it simply become struck by the leprosy of which they will cure the world.

SATURDAY

Now the word of the Lord came to Jonah, saying, Arise, go to Nineveh (Jonah 1 : 1–2).

JONAH AND THE NINEVITES

A third incident to which Jesus refers in His preaching to show what God is like and how in God's purposes men are related to one another, is the story of Jonah (Matt. 12 : 38–41). In the story, when finally Jonah finds that God has forgiven Nineveh and spared it, Jonah breaks out in angry expostulation and says, 'I was not willing, in the first place, to do what you asked me to do because I knew you. I knew that you were a gracious and merciful God and that, therefore, in spite of the fact that I had announced destruction on Nineveh at your command, you would change your own mind and forgive instead of destroy. Therefore, now let me die. I cannot live any longer as your prophet. You have let me down.' It has been truly said that no one should preach judgement except with a sob in his voice. When Jesus announced the destruction of Jerusalem, He wept. The heart of Jonah's problem is that he knows his God, but does not approve.

In the body of the story of Jonah, we see what the consequences are for others of the kind of man Jonah was. He is on a merchant ship going on a normal trading voyage. The result for the merchants of having Jonah aboard is that they run into an unexpected storm and lose all their merchandise and come very close also to losing their lives. A disobedient Church is a menace to the world. It is others who suffer when those who must carry the message of God refuse to carry it. In the story of Paul on his voyage to Rome, the missionary was the means of saving the lives of those who sailed with him. In Jonah's story, the disobedient missionary has become a menace. The merchantmen, when they discovered Jonah, threw him into the sea. There was nothing else they could do. That was the only way they had to protect themselves. How often, in the history of the Church across the centuries this has happened, that God has used the world to bring back the Church to Him.

When Jonah is cast into the sea, he is at God's mercy. God has prepared a great fish to swallow him and in that fish, alone for three days and three nights, Jonah finds his will to obedience again. The irony of the story is that whereas Jonah knew in his own life and through his own experience how gracious God was, he was not willing that that graciousness should be extended over Nineveh also.

When the people of Nineveh heard the message of Jonah, they repented. 'Let everyone turn from his evil way'—so ran the King's proclamation. 'Who knows, God may yet repent and turn from His fierce anger, so that we perish not?' The King of Nineveh and his people were not worshippers of Yahweh and yet they understood the import of the message which Jonah brought. It is to this fact that Jesus primarily refers when He uses this story to answer the question of the scribes and Pharisees. They asked Him for a sign. He says to them, 'What sign did the men of Nineveh get? Did they not, even though they were not children of Israel, repent at the preaching of Jonah? If they found the preaching of Jonah enough, why are you not satisfied with my preaching? A greater than Jonah is here. The very search for a sign is proof that you are an adulterous people. You do not know who your true Lord is. When that is your problem, no external sign will solve it' (Luke 11 : 29–30).

At no time can the Church give to the world any other sign except the word it proclaims and itself as a sign and proof of God's mercy. That in spite of our disobedience, God yet trusts us with His word is proof enough of the graciousness of God to all men.

THE FOURTH WEEK IN LENT

What are the ethical imperatives of the Christian life? It is simple enough to say that law is abrogated by grace. However, is that true? What grace does is to change the function of law. Instead of being looked upon as a means of procuring God's favour, law assumes the role of being a means of showing our gratitude. What do the 'do's' and 'don'ts' of the Christian life look like in this perspective?

The particular relationships that are dealt with in the studies for this week are intended also to show the ways in which Christian ethical thinking is conducted.

SUNDAY

Called to belong to Jesus Christ (Rom. 1 : 6).

OUR WAY WITH ONE ANOTHER

Our study this week is to be on the living of the Christian life in the several relationships in which we have to live it. As an introduction to this study, our first attempt will be to find out how the Bible helps us to think about this kind of question. When we turn to Scripture and ask how can we get from it the guidance we need for personal ethical living, what answer do we get?

We must begin by reminding ourselves that the Scriptures are a testimony to Jesus and are intended to persuade us to believe in Him and to have life in His name. Personal ethical living begins there. It is the consequence of being in Christ, members of His Body, branches that abide in the Vine. As it says in the prologue to John's gospel, 'As many as came to him, to them he opened a way, to become children of God' (John 1:12). Through Jesus Christ a new possibility of existence has been opened up for men. In a very literal sense, it has become possible to live in Jesus Christ, to live within Him. Paul's phrase 'in Christ' is practically synonymous with the phrase 'in the Church', 'in the Body of Christ'. The Church, as we have seen already, is the place where the healing processes of Christ are at work.

Thus, before we can talk about the responsibility of a Christian for personal ethical living, we must insist that this person be a Christian, that is, a person who is in Christ. This involves two things: first, that he be in the family of the Church, and that he learn daily more and more to take his place within the family, identifying himself with it, and accepting all its members as people whom he cannot reject. You cannot pick and choose your brothers and sisters: they belong. Secondly, we must realize that Christianity today is a separate religion only because Jesus rose from the dead; and one consequence of the resurrection is that we can meet Him. In other words, if we have never met Him, the question of Christian ethical living will not arise for us.

But what is the relationship of the Bible to this? The Bible is the place where we meet the Lord, where we hear Him speak to us, where we meet the community of saints. J. B. Phillips, in his preface to the paraphrase he made of the epistles, says that he felt as if he were trying to mend an electric light system without being able to shut off the current. Whenever we handle the Bible, we get that feeling. This is not a dead book; it is alive, and we may get a shock at any time.

Personal Christian ethical living, then, is the consequence of something having happened to us. It is a 'therefore'. 'I am the Lord, your God, who brought you out of the land of Egypt; therefore, you shall have no other gods before me; therefore, you shall honour your father and mother; therefore, you shall not commit adultery' (Ex. 20:2f). The Ten Commandments are a 'therefore'. 'Hear, O Israel; the Lord our God is one Lord; and you shall love the Lord your God with all your heart, and with all your soul, and with all your might' (Deut. 6:4). The command arises out of the previous truth that God has acted on Israel's behalf, making himself her God. 'Behave in such a way', said Jesus, 'that you may be children of your Father who is in heaven' (Matt. 5:45). The ethical demands are made and understood in terms of who we are. These demands are made of us because we are His children, called to belong to Jesus Christ, redeemed by Him, and enlisted as soldiers in His service.

We commonly speak of the Christian life as beginning with an experience of conversion. Conversion is not deciding to be good or deciding to be saved, but deciding to be His. This is also why 'holy living' cannot be a solo experience. Each one, who has decided to be His, is His within the Church, within the community of those who belong. It is this Church, this community, that is to be presented to Christ as 'a Bride without blemish' (Eph. 5:27). The whole affair is plural in intention and implication.

What forms, then, does the Christian ethical demand take for us as persons? There are six different areas to be distinguished in the answer which must be given.

A converted life. The first area is defined by the scriptural injunction, 'You have passed from darkness to light; therefore, give up the works of darkness. Do not steal. Do not commit adultery. Do not covet. And so forth' (1 Pet. 2 :9). Of course, the demand that men give up evil ways is a demand which is true of all religions. One does not have to be a Christian to be told, 'Do not steal'. The only difference is that for Christians the moral life is a 'therefore'. 'Therefore', says Paul, 'I appeal to you to present your bodies as a living sacrifice' (Rom. 12 :1).

The personal equation. The second area in which the ethical demand comes to us is that of our own particular nature. Each of us is made differently. Each has his own weakness and temptations, and each has to deal with the ethical demand in terms of himself. It is true that Jesus said, 'I came that they may have life, and have it abundantly'; but He also said, 'If your eye offend you, pluck it out; if your hand offend you, cut it off' (Mark 9 :43f). When one meets a person who has never found it necessary to perform any of these surgical operations on himself, one begins to wonder whether he is living the ethical life. There is some part of the life of every person of which Jesus says, 'Pluck it out, cut it off. It is much better that this particular weakness should be completely eradicated than that you should simply seek grace to deal with it.' If a man who is rather poor becomes a treasurer of the church, he will be tempted to take church money for his own use, hoping to replace it the next month. Then he may be unable to replace it the next month, and only with some difficulty is the matter put right. He will go through this process again and again. It will be much better for him to refuse to be the treasurer of public funds, than to say, 'God will give me grace to overcome this temptation'. There are always certain temptations which it is better for us never to face. I have a feeling that one of Paul's areas of difficulty was that he did not know how to get along with women. So he never got married—a very sensible course. Each has to find out for himself where his weaknesses lie, and what surgical operations he must perform on his own life.

The soldier's discipline. The third area is that which is concerned with the discipline of the soldier. Paul in his letter to Timothy says, 'No soldier on service gets entangled in civilian pursuits' (2 Tim. 2:4). We are all soldiers and are, therefore, involved in the positive and the negative disciplines of soldiering. The positive is easy enough to explain. One of the main things a soldier must do is to keep in contact with his commander; otherwise he will not receive orders, he will not know what to do. A Christian soldier must keep up his prayer life and his Bible study. He must be regular at church and in the life of the Christian fellowship. The negative discipline is equally important. Many Christians find time and money for everything that other people are also interested in. For example, I am a Christian and my next-door neighbour is a Hindu. He is a good man, a religious man. I am the same kind of person. I earn about the same amount of money as he does. His children go to the pictures so many times a week; my children go the same number of times. He has time to do this and that. I have time for the same things. I am able to live the same normal life that everyone else lives and, with the balance of money and time I have, I want to serve the kingdom of God. It cannot be done. The Bible says that I cannot expect to do this. In other words, the soldier's life demands that I learn to give up good things and not only bad things; and it is in giving up the good things that the problems arise. Jesus told a story about a man who spent a good deal of time and trouble collecting pearls. When he had collected a large number, he came across a big pearl. He sold all the pearls that he had in order to get the pearl of great price (Matt. 13:45-46). It is not uncommon to meet with Christian people who say, 'But why should I give it up, it is a pearl.' Of course it is a pearl. But one has to give it up if one wants the other pearl.

For brethren's sake. The fourth area from which the demand comes to us for personal ethical living is that of renunciation for the sake of those to whom we seek to commend the gospel. To use the Pauline phrase, 'in order that the brother for whom Jesus died may not stumble' (Rom. 14:15). There are certain things which I must not do, not because it will do me any harm, but because it will harm the person whom I am trying to win for Jesus Christ. Let me give an example. In the *ashram* we have in Ceylon, everyone is a vegetarian, because the *ashram* is open to anyone who wants to come, and many Hindus who are vegetarians will come. Of course there is nothing harmful or sinful in eating meat, and one may say that the Christian ought somehow to tell the Hindu that there is no harm in it. I remember my father telling me about the missionaries of his day saying, 'So-and-so is very near conversion because he has begun to eat mutton.' I was born and brought up in Ceylon. When I first came to Europe some years ago, I went to the home of Pierre Maury for a meal. He produced wine. I said, 'I don't drink wine', and he said, 'Well, Niles, you don't know the freedom of the gospel.' It may be one's Christian duty in France to teach people that it is possible to drink in moderation. It certainly is not in Ceylon. There are certain renunciations in which one is involved because one wants to commend the gospel to a particular group of people.

Vocation and its demands. Fifthly, there are the disciplines in which we are involved because of our special callings in the Christian Church. I am a preacher. I must study, I must have a certain amount of time every day

84

for my books, for my study of the Bible, for my Greek which once I learned at college. There will be another discipline involved if one finds oneself taking part in the healing ministry of the Church. It is a discipline that the person must find for himself. I have a friend, an Anglican minister, who joined the Guild of Healing of the Church and who used to hold healing services with anointing and the laying on of hands. He said to me one day, 'You know that I have normally used a certain amount of liquor as a beverage along with my meals. There is nothing wrong or sinful about it. But I find that I have to give it up, if I am to engage in this ministry of healing.' It is no good asking him for theological reasons. The whole point of personal living is that it is personal. It is the kind of thing that you are involved in because you are you, and your own vocation makes its specific demands.

In obedience to the cross. Lastly, there is the problem of carrying the cross. By the cross is not meant the problems, the difficulties, the dangers we encounter as the result of living the Christian life. The cross of Jesus was the result of His insisting on loving people who said to Him, 'We don't want to have anything to do with you, get out.' The cross is the result of love as the response to rejection. If we have reached the place where everyone accepts us, then Jesus says, 'Woe unto you', because then we have escaped the cross. We have somehow adjusted ourselves to everybody so that we move smoothly and do not have to face the cross. Jesus says if you are that kind of person there is something very seriously wrong with you (Luke 6:26). This does not mean that we must make ourselves as unpleasant as possible, so that people will say, 'We don't want to have anything to do with you, get out'. But any Christian will normally come up against situations where either a person or a group will say, 'I want to have nothing to do with you, get out.' Should I face such rejection and answer that rejection with love, then there will be a cross to carry. The problem of ethical living at this point becomes very difficult indeed. For it is very difficult to carry one's cross without feeling what a good fellow one is!

The Bible, then, does not give rules or principles for all these areas where we meet with ethical demands. All it does is to fix the climate in which we live, and to teach us that we must learn to live without feeling either religious or moral. Indeed, the whole nature of the ethical life as the Christian must live it is misunderstood when it is understood in religious or moral terms. Its true point of reference is that into this world in which we have to live this life God has come in Jesus Christ; and that He continues to live in it through Christ's risen life, thus setting up at the centre of life a whirlpool caused by His activity—activity in the life of a community established by His call and over all life through the pressures of His advancing kingdom.

How does one set about living this kind of life? I think all of us have glimpsed the answer now and again in our own lives. It is to maintain within one's life, at the centre of it if possible, an area of freedom, to learn to live fundamentally in the passive rather than the active voice, so that the quality of life is determined essentially not by what we do but by what we are. A home is a very good example of a place where people normally, naturally, live in the passive voice. A husband does not live in the active voice, behaving as a person who is obliged to love his wife and children. He lives in the passive voice as a person who is loved by his wife and children. My children do not get up in the morning and say, 'Now today we must love father and mother.' They simply behave as people who are loved by father and mother. It is because, at home, everyone lives in the passive voice that the demands of the home are met. Ethical living becomes possible because it is never attempted. It simply results from the fact that the centre of the home is an area of complete inner freedom. If our Christian life can be built, not on the basis of 'I must love God and my neighbour', but of 'God loves me, and my neighbour', then the ethical demand can be met without our saying to ourselves, 'I am an ethical person.' Could this be what Jesus meant when He said, 'Having done all that is commanded of you, say, we are unworthy servants' (Luke 17:10).

MONDAY

Children, obey your parents in the Lord
(Eph. 6:1–4).

PARENTS AND CHILDREN

'In the Lord' is the definitive phrase in this passage. In describing the relation which should exist between Christian parents and children, Paul is not intending to describe a purely biological relationship or even a purely natural one. Christian parents and their children belong to one another in Jesus Christ. As Paul himself explains it, in his letter to the Corinthians, those who participate in Jesus Christ participate in His death. The result is that all relationships after the flesh are dissolved and the new relationships which are set up, are set up in Christ. So that when it is said that parents and children belong to one another in the Lord, it is emphasized that the consequences of the relationship must be controlled by the love of Christ (2 Cor. 5 : 14–16). The sign among the people of Israel that they belonged to the Lord was the sign of circumcision. To be circumcised was to accept that procreation was no independent right of man, and that his children belonged to God.

The first obligation, within this relationship of parents to children, which Paul mentions, is that of children obeying their parents. He refers to the fact that the first commandment, in the series of commandments which deals with man's relationship with man, is the commandment to honour one's father and mother. The word 'honour' is not the same as the word 'obey'. To honour is to acknowledge the rights of one's parents to one's loyalty and love. It is dishonourable for a child, for instance, to do secretly what it knows its parents will disapprove. It may be that the child has the right to do what it wants, but it has no right to do it secretly. For the word 'obey' which Paul uses has also the qualifying phrase, 'in the Lord'. This means that where there is disobedience, it too has to be 'in the Lord'. It must be the consequence of being controlled by Christ's love.

Paul makes a further point, by referring to the promise attached to the Old Testament commandment—'that it may be well with you and that you may live long on the earth'. In the evils which are listed in Romans 1 : 30 and 2 Timothy 3 : 2, as contributing to the disintegration of society, disobedience to parents finds a place. To put it at its lowest level, the wisdom of experience is one of the safest guides that the young can get, and to discard it is one of the surest ways of seeking trouble.

The parallel obligation which Paul imposes on parents is that they should not provoke their children to anger. J. B. Phillips in his paraphrase writes, 'Do not over-correct your children.' When a child knows that what he is doing is wrong, it is not necessary after that to point it out. It is enough for him to know that his parents know and that they appreciate his determination to do right next time. To over-correct is to keep rubbing in what does not need to be rubbed in. In his letter to the Colossians, Paul writes, 'Fathers, do not provoke your children, lest they become discouraged.' Often, parents administer correction in order to fashion the child's life in terms of their own decisions for him. An ambitious father wants his son to become a doctor, or an anxious mother wants her daughter to get married soon. The all-important question is, however—what is the direction of the child's own life? What is the child becoming in the Lord? When correction keeps constantly thwarting the inner direction of a child's own life, it becomes discouraged. Besides, as Paul has it in his letter to the Ephesians, the warning must go even beyond this; for parents can not only discourage their children, they can even drive them to anger. No correction of a child is worth it, if the relationship between child and parent is broken thereby. Parents need to be careful to see that their children never resent them. They must remember that they are the first means by which the child is loved by God, and they must take trouble to let the child see their permanent affection for it.

It is not possible to leave this subject speaking only of parents in general or of fathers in particular. Paul makes no reference to mothers as such, but a special role which mothers fulfil has to be emphasized. There is a sense in which a child always treats its mother as an equal; and, particularly during its early years, the child constantly tests its will against the will of its mother. That is the way in which the individuality of the child grows and the child comes to know itself as a person. That is also the way in which the child finds out the extent and limitations of its freedom. In the last analysis, this freedom is defined both for child and parent, both in its extent and its limitations, by the love of God for them in Jesus Christ.

TUESDAY

Be subject to one another out of reverence for Christ (Eph. 5 : 21–23).

HUSBANDS AND WIVES

Just as in dealing with the relation between parents and children, Paul bases his teaching on the relation between God who is Father and every home which derives its name and nature from Him (Eph. 3 : 15), even so in dealing with the relation between husbands and wives, he bases his teaching on the relation between Christ and His Church.

The first implication of this analogy is that wives must be subject to their husbands, for the husband is the head of the wife as Christ is the head of the Church. This injunction, however, is set within two limits. The first limit is found in the fact that 'to be subject' is a mutual relation that Christians bear to one another out of reverence for Christ. In other words, the special injunction that wives be subject to their husbands does not do away with the general relation in which husbands also need to learn to be subject to their wives. The second limit is found in the fact that Christ is not only the head of the Church, but is also its Saviour. So that subjection of wife to husband is held within a saving relationship in which the husband's attitude to the wife has to be one of patient love and consideration.

In Peter's first epistle (3 : 1–7), the first emphasis, in describing the relation between wife and husband, falls on the wife's role as saviour. The wife must win her husband for the Lord. The way to do this is for the wife to maintain towards her husband the attitude that she should maintain before God. She must be known for her reverent and chaste behaviour, for her gentle and quiet spirit. A woman, says Peter, gains nothing, as far as her husband is concerned, by any kind of outward adorning. As for the attitude of husbands to their wives, Peter describes it as consisting in living considerately and bestowing honour on her as the weaker vessel. A precious vase must be handled carefully and delicately. If one is rough with it, it will break. The advice is also given to wives that even if the husbands are rough with them, they should not allow themselves to be terrified. 'Be not afraid', he says, 'with a fear that flutters.' The mutuality in which husbands and wives belong to one another is finally emphasized by Peter in the pregnant saying, 'You are joint heirs of the grace of life.' Here is a sacramental relation in which the wife administers the sacrament of life to her husband and the husband administers the sacrament of life to his wife. Should this mutual relationship be destroyed by the husband's lack of consideration for his wife, whereby he drives her to tears, then says Peter, 'his prayers will never reach God'.

As we meditate on what Paul and Peter are both saying, we become aware that they are not merely speaking of the experience of husbands and wives in their relationship to one another. They are saying rather that the relationship between husbands and wives is one of the ways of entering into the relationship between Christ and His Church. Here is more than an analogy. The lesser depends on the greater and affords an entrance into the greater, while the greater sustains the lesser and makes it possible.

*Whatever good anyone does, he will receive the
same again from the Lord, whether he is a slave
or free* (Eph. 6 :8).

MASTERS AND SERVANTS

The slave has no rights, so that the emphasis falls on the
nature of the inner attitudes which must be maintained
between master and servant. The first injunction given
is that a man, whether slave or free, must accept the work
which he has to do as service rendered to the Lord.
Therefore, it must be done thoroughly and heartily. But
what is the point of that, a slave might say, for however
well I do my work, there is nothing due to me. I am
only a slave. Why not then do my work in such a way
that it is just passable? Paul's answer is to say that,
whether slave or free, it is God who rewards work done.
We, too, are slaves of Christ, and as slaves there is nothing
due to us as reward for our work from our Master.
Salvation is a gift of pure grace and is never a reward for
service rendered. And yet, it is precisely because salvation
is by grace alone that we work for Him, who has saved
us, heartily and with all that we can put into our work.
What then of the problem of injustice? For masters are
often unjust to their slaves. Peter, in dealing with this
question, makes the point that in the calling of the
Christian to share in the cross of Christ is included his
calling to bear injustice even as Christ bore it. There is no
condoning of injustice as such. What Peter wants those
who suffer injustice to do is to remember that thereby they
are afforded a privilege which they must cherish (1 Pet.
2 : 18–25).

Paul opens his injunction to masters with the surprising

statement, 'Do the same to them.' Not only must servants serve their master, but the master must also serve his servants. The example of Christ must be followed, who though He was Master still lived among men as He who served. Masters must also forbear from threatening their servants. The servant may be a slave; nevertheless, he is not ultimately at his master's mercy. Jesus Christ is Master both of masters and servants, and they equally belong to Him.

There is no teaching in Scripture which is more emphasized than this, that God is the God of the helpless, of the marginal person in society. He will inquire into and bring to judgement the ways in which the widow, the fatherless, the stranger, the poor are treated. It is not by accident that, in the parable of the last judgement, the persons mentioned by our Lord are all persons who are marginal in society—those who are hungry and thirsty because they are poor, those who have no home because they are strangers, and those whom society itself has segregated and put into prison.

The final warning of Paul, both to masters and servants, is that there is no partiality with God. It will always be true of both groups that with what measure they measure, it will be measured to them again. Let the attitude of the servant to his master reflect the attitude that he must have also to his Master Jesus Christ. And let the attitude of masters to servants reflect the attitude of Jesus Christ to all those who serve Him. The analogy of the relation between masters and servants is that of the relation between Jesus Christ and those who are engaged in His service.

THURSDAY

*A new commandment I give to you, that you
love one another; even as I have loved you*
(John 13 :34).

CHRISTIAN AND FELLOW CHRISTIAN

There are three commandments which define for the
Christian the obligation which he bears in love. The first
commandment is to love God. But since love has only
one origin and that is God himself, our love for Him
springs from His love for us. The emphasis that God
first loved us is not simply an emphasis of the fact that
He loved us before we loved Him. This is true. For there
was nothing we had done which made Him love us. He
loved us as we were and in spite of ourselves. The thrust,
however, of the statement that He first loved us goes
even beyond this. It is the recognition of the fact that
He has to love us first if we are to love Him at all. Our
love is always love in response; it is His love which creates
ours.

The second commandment is that we love our neighbour as we love ourselves. We love ourselves for no reason
whatever. No woman loves herself because she is beautiful. No man loves himself because he is wise or rich. The
command then is that even as there is no reason which we
find good enough not to love ourselves, even so there is no
reason good enough not to love our neighbour. Is this
kind of love possible? It becomes possible when we see
our neighbour as he truly is, as someone whom God loves.
My love for my neighbour is no more than God's love for
him through me. Also, God comes to me in my neighbour, so that my love for him is no more than my love for
God as He comes to me in him (Luke 10 :27).

94

The Christian is bound by a third commandment also : 'Love one another even as I have loved you.' Christ has loved us together, so that Christian and fellow-Christian are bound, each to other, by a love which encompasses them both. To betray this love for each other is to deny His love by which both are bound. John, in his epistle, recognizes how difficult, even surprising, this kind of love can be between the brethren. That is why he says, 'We know that we have passed out of death into life because we love the brethren' (1 John 3 : 14). In other words, when we find that we are able, without reserve, to love those who belong with us in the fellowship of those who bear the name of Christ, then we know that something has happened to us. We know that God's love for us in Jesus Christ has removed us out of the realm of death into the realm of life. To hate someone is a death-relationship. To love someone is a life-relationship. But there is no way of passing from death to life, except through response to the life-giving love of God in Jesus Christ.

Peter, writing on the love of the brethren, says, 'Do not return evil for evil or reviling for reviling, but on the contrary bless, for to this you have been called that you may obtain a blessing' (1 Peter. 3:9). A simple implication of what Peter says is that we should learn to give to others out of what God gives to us. Since it is blessing which we have received from God, let us bless. Should one want to revile or do evil to another, these have to be first received in order to be passed on, and the only source from which we can receive these is the devil. To abide in death is to keep the devil as the source of our supply.

And I have other sheep, that are not of this fold; I must bring them also (John 10:16).

CHRISTIAN AND NON-CHRISTIAN

The word 'non-Christian' is a word in common usage, but it is a word difficult to justify in terms of the Christian faith. When we say that somebody is a non-Christian, the force of the epithet is to qualify. It is adjectival in its implication. But is there anyone of whom this can be said? Are not all men within the love and ministry of God in Jesus Christ and the Holy Spirit? God made all men. God loves all men. All men are within His providence. For all men Jesus died. In all men God's Spirit is at work. All men, at the end, will be judged by Jesus Christ. These things are all true of all men whether they know it or not, like it or not, accept it or not. It is possible to say, it is necessary to say, So-and-so is not a Christian. However, the phrase, 'not a Christian', is verbal in its force and not adjectival. It simply states what a certain person has done or not done. When we say that a person is not a Christian, we are only saying that he does not acknowledge Jesus Christ as Lord. We do not deny that he is within the Lordship of Jesus Christ.

In the relationship, therefore, which Christians must maintain with those who are not Christians, there must be the attempt both to express the exclusiveness and the inclusiveness of the Christian faith. It is essential that men must be helped to know who they truly are and to respond consciously to what God has done for them in Jesus Christ. Let me use an illustration which, while it does not apply to the reasons why men do not acknowledge Jesus Christ, still illustrates the importance of such acknowledgement. I saw a picture once of an idiot child with its mother kneeling beside it, her arms around her child and on her face a look of great sadness. Underneath was the caption, 'He does not know'. That the child did not know his mother did not alter the fact that she was the mother or that she loved; but that the child did not know prevented that love from finding its fulfilment. Whatever the reason be that men do not know or do not acknowledge God's love for them in Jesus Christ, where such acknowledgement is lacking, this love of God lacks fulfilment. But where there is this fulfilment, there this love is released in multiplying force in the life of the person concerned and in the lives of those to whom he is related.

No Christian can adopt an attitude to those who are not Christians, which is based on the assumption that this kind of acknowledgement is optional or unnecessary : and yet this must not mean that the inclusiveness of the Christian faith is forgotten. One's primary attitude to a person who is not a Christian is not to look upon him as a prospective convert. There must be full recognition that he or she is already within the saving ministry of Christ. It is when this attitude is maintained that it is possible to enter into conversation with a person who is not a Christian expecting to hear from his evidence of the ways in which God has been at work in his life. We are so often so anxious to tell others about Jesus Christ, that we do not listen to what they have to tell us about Him, even though they do not know that it is about Him they are speaking.

When Jesus said to His disciples, 'All authority has been given to me in heaven and on earth, therefore go into all the world (Matt. 28:18–19), He was saying that they could go anywhere and to anyone because everywhere and over everyone He was already in authority. All men, both Christians and those who are not, are already related to one another within the Lordship of Jesus Christ.

Being very eager to write to you of our common salvation, I found it necessary to write appealing to you to contend for the faith (Jude 3).

BELIEVER AND UNBELIEVER

It is inevitable that when life has to be lived together, there would always be those who belong but who nevertheless do not believe. The letter of Jude is concerned with this problem. He says, 'Ungodly persons have surreptitiously entered the Church. They have no real reverence for God, and they abuse His grace as an opportunity for immorality. They will not recognize the only Master—Jesus Christ our Lord. Because of them, those who do believe must constantly be alert contending for the faith committed to those who belong to Christ.'

In describing those with whom the faithful must contend, Jude uses some striking pictures. They are as clouds which carry no rain, as trees in autumn which carry no fruit, as waves of the sea whose movement only churns up foam, as stars which have no direction. These people will appear among the faithful as those who scoff, making a joke of everything in which the faithful believe. They will do this not so much by poking fun, but by acting as if the things believed in are of no account. The consequence of who they are and the attitude they adopt will be to produce divisions in the Church and to cause wranglings and quarrels and dissensions.

'You therefore,' says Jude to the faithful, 'will need not only to protect yourself, but also to deal as Christianly as can be with these others. In order to protect yourself, you must do three things. You must send down the roots of your life into your faith, getting strong nourishment thereby. You must also learn to pray in the Holy Spirit, so that you keep yourselves within the love of God. And finally, wait patiently for the mercy of Jesus Christ which will bring you to the life eternal.'

There is a great deal in life to make faith difficult. The faithless around you will be constantly pointing to them, so that faith has to be anchored at a much deeper level than the experiences that lie on the surface. But not only will faith be tested, love will be tested also. It will be difficult to maintain one's love towards God as well as to rest in God's love towards oneself. It will often look as if the obligation to love and the experience of being loved lead nowhere. All the more reason then to be fully responsive to the work of the Holy Spirit in one's life. There will be the temptation, too, to give up hope. Things do not change as fast as we hope they would. God will seem not to care. But the believer will learn to wait patiently. He knows that he is waiting for the mercy of Jesus Christ—a mercy which, if it is not too early, is never too late. Wait then for God's time. For, He will do for you that which is of eternal moment, dealing with you and with your problems, at the right time, in ways which will secure for you your spiritual destiny. 'You, the faithful,' Jude says, 'have also a duty to the others, a duty which goes beyond just contending with them. Among these others will be those whose ungodliness is no more than doubt about the feasibility of living by God alone. These need to be convinced by your faith. Some are just weak and helpless. These you can save, snatching them as it were out of the fire. While some are actually evil-doers. However, these too can be won. Only, in their case, you need to be afraid of them to the extent that you do not get too close to them. However, coupled with your fear of them, there must be also sympathy for them—show them mercy.'

Life in the plural can never be a straightforward affair. It is bound to be full of turmoil and temptation. But God can keep us from falling and present us without blemish before the presence of His glory with rejoicing.

THE FIFTH WEEK IN LENT

Morality and religion belong together in an indivisible whole. Our way with one another is firmly wedged within His way with us. During this week, we shall probe further into this interlocking relationship.

The experiences and situations which have been chosen for the six meditations are in no way exhaustive or even definitive of the experience of God in our lives. They can only be illustrative. That is why there are a variety of themes in the choice made.

Sunday

Truly, thou art a God who hidest thyself, O God of Israel, the saviour (Is. 45:15).

HIS WAY WITH US

What are the ways of God with men? There can never be an adequate answer to this question. We can only see the wrong side of the tapestry. And yet, men must have an answer adequate to live by and to live with. There is a key concept in the Scriptures which, it seems to me, we can use as a window through which to look, in order that we may get some understanding of why God's ways with men are such as they are.

When the Israelites were exiles in Babylon, they maintained for some time, undimmed, their hope that God would deliver them and restore them to their own land. But soon hope ran out, giving place to a mood of settled sorrow. A good example of this mood is in Psalm 137. Jerusalem is not forgotten, but the remembrance of Jerusalem does not enkindle hope.

> 'By the waters of Babylon,
>   there we sat down and wept,
>   When we remembered Zion.
> On the willows there
>   we hung up our lyres.
> How shall we sing the Lord's song
>   in a foreign land?'

But soon, sooner than Israel had expected, they were on their way back to Jerusalem. The empire of Babylon had gone, and Cyrus, the Persian, had set them free. The surprise of this event finds joyous expression in another psalm (126):

> 'When the Lord restored the fortunes of Zion,
>   we were like those who dream.
> Then our mouth was filled with laughter,
>   and our tongue with shouts of joy;
> then they said among the nations,
>   The Lord has done great things for them.'

The prophet's comment on this experience was to say, 'Truly thou art a God who hidest thyself, O God of Israel, the saviour.'

In the second epistle of Peter, we read of scoffers who will say, 'Where is the promise of his coming? For ever since the fathers fell asleep, all things have continued as they were from the beginning of creation' (3:4). And the reply given is to say, 'With the Lord one day is as a thousand years and a thousand years as one day.' God will do in one day what it takes a thousand years to do, even though it may seem that for a thousand years He has kept quiet. 'He will come,' says the writer, 'like a thief.'

But why does he come so furtively and quietly? Why is it, to use the prophet's words, that God hides himself, so that it is so difficult to know what He is doing and so difficult to know when He will do what He has promised to do? It is always dangerous to say that the reasons why God does what He does are the same as the consequences to us of His way of doing them. And yet, it is only the consequences that we know, consequences which determine for us the ways in which we understand God and, therefore, the ways in which we seek to live with Him.

One consequence of the hiddenness of God is that it strengthens faith. We learn to trust Him under all appearances. The Son of God walked the earth as a wandering preacher. He died like a felon on a cross. But in that death was hidden the salvation of the world. Because He hides himself, faith remains alert and probing. Had angels come to His rescue at Gethsemane, there would have been an open demonstration of the power of God (Matt. 26 : 53). As it was, no angels intervened. But when the time came, Jesus rose from the dead. God must hide himself, if we are to live by faith.

Not only does God demand faith, but He asks also to be treasured. Jesus said, 'You must not cast pearls before swine' (Matt. 7 : 6). There must be that appreciation of God's wealth which makes us seek and keep on seeking, that appreciation of God's presence which makes us knock and keep on knocking, that appreciation of God's promises which makes us ask and keep on asking (Matt. 7 : 7). God does not indulge us with an open display of all that He can do. He waits till we really want. There is a Hindu story which speaks of a man who wanted to see God. He went to a *rishi* with his request. The *rishi* took him to a river, submerged him in it, and after some time, when he came out spluttering, said to him, 'When you want to meet God as badly as you wanted air when I held you under the water, then you will meet Him.'

God has decided also that His gifts must be worked for. He hides electricity in the waterfall, and coal and oil in the ground. We must mine for the coal, dig for the oil, harness the water to get electric power. It is equally true that often God's answers to our prayers are hidden in other people. These people have to be welcomed into our lives before we find the answer. We may have to work with them, we may have to forgive them, we may have to make requests of them before we can receive what God has hidden for us in them. Jesus told us a parable about a man who went to plough and found a treasure (Matt. 13 :44). The treasure was not the result of his ploughing. God had hidden it there. But the man would never have found it unless he had gone to plough. What God will do for us is never determined by what we do; and yet what we do is an integral part of the way we must take if we are to find what He has hidden for us.

God is also working to produce beauty. There is the story of a naturalist who was examining a chrysalis. The emerging butterfly seemed to be in great difficulties. It seemed unable to win its freedom. The naturalist took his knife and cut the chrysalis open, only to find that while the butterfly emerged without a struggle, there were no colours on its wings. I have a piece of beautiful timber with a wonderful grain on it. Friends in New Zealand gave it to me. They said that the tree from which this timber came was a tree with a soft bark. When the winds blew and raised the sands, the sands struck against the soft bark and made the beautiful grain of the tree. Beauty is always the result of struggle. God knows it and, therefore, does not spare His children the struggles which they must go through; nor does He spare himself the anxiety He must feel concerning our struggles. There is an Arab proverb which says 'Sunshine makes the desert'. The long and hard winters are part of the scheme of life. Without them, life does become a desert. It is part of the wisdom of the hiding ministries of heaven that there shall be both sun and rain, summer and winter.

And finally, God hides himself because we cannot bear Him. It is by His mercy that His tears, on account of our sinfulness and waywardness, are hidden in the heartache of a mother, the anxiety of a friend, and the troublings of one's own conscience. Should God show himself directly to us, and as He truly thinks of us, we could not survive it.

However, our meditation on the hiddenness of God cannot stop here. For what we have really done is to think of it in the ways in which we normally experience it. We must return to look at what the prophet himself is saying in the context in which he says it. The context is the deliverance wrought for Israel by God through Cyrus, so that the prophet makes God say to Cyrus,

'I call you by your name,
I surname you, though you do not know me,
I am the Lord, and there is no other,
Beside me, there is no God' (Is. 45:4–5).

When Pandit Jawaharlal Nehru died, the *Christian News Bulletin* in Ceylon said that, inasmuch as he was not a Christian, his life and service were a challenge to Christian faith. Is this not an exact opposite of the truth? It is men like Nehru who point to the greatness of our God whose grace is seen as it works through men who do not acknowledge His name. There, in the life of that great statesman, was the hiddenness of God. That men like Nehru explained their lives in other terms does not challenge the faith of the Christian. What is exposed is the failure of Christians so to communicate the faith that men see whom it is that they really serve and who it is to whom they really belong.

In the passage already quoted from Isaiah, the reason given for this way of God in the world is expressed with straightforward simplicity. It is, the prophet says, 'For the sake of my servant Jacob, and Israel my chosen'. In its immediate context, the prophet's reference is to Cyrus through whom God worked to deliver His people from exile; but the insight to which the prophet gives expression is wider-ranging in its implications. It is because God maintains His Lordship over the world, that they who acknowledge Him are able to witness to Him as Lord. It is also because the fulfilment of God's purposes in the world is not tied to the obedience of those who know and confess Him, that they themselves are not left at the mercy of their own works. Because He remains Lord, they are able to point to Him without having to point to themselves also.

MONDAY

My grace is sufficient for you (2 Cor. 12 :9).

THE MINISTRY OF PAIN

Among the commonest experiences of life is the experience of pain; and never is the question 'Why?' more insistent than when pain comes. Is it God who is doing this to me? Why is He doing it? And, if it is not God, what is He doing about it? It is essential to recognize that there are no real answers to these questions—real in the sense that there is any way by which we can enter into the mind of God and understand what He is doing and why. And yet, we know enough of God's ways with men to rest in Him. What do we know?

We know, first of all, that the experience of pain belongs to this world. When Sir Henry De Mel, the father of the present Metropolitan of Calcutta was shot and killed by a young man whom he himself had brought up, I wrote a letter of sympathy to his son, then a priest in Ceylon. In replying to me he said, 'This is the kind of world in which these kinds of things happen.' We must learn to accept this world as it is. Those who wrote the book of Deuteronomy created for themselves a simple frame of reference within which to explain misfortune and disaster. If one was righteous before God, one was blessed. If one was unrighteous, one was punished. The difference between the righteous and the unrighteous lay in whether one worshipped the true God or not. Paul, in his letter to the Romans, takes us much beyond Deuteronomy. He says quite simply, 'None is righteous, no, not one' (Rom. 3:10). Life in the world is life amidst the working out of secondary causes. God, indeed, remains the primary cause, but there is no way of relating what happens in this world directly to Him. It is, of course, necessary and possible to qualify what has been said in order to maintain the truth of the possibility of miracle and the efficacy of prayer. But this truth should never be so stated or believed in as to qualify our acceptance of this world as it is.

Secondly, there is always the fact that we know that God is busy with us—each one knows how in his own life : so that when pain comes, it is legitimate to think of the ministry of pain. Paul talks about the ways in which God tests us, but never more than we are able to bear (1 Cor. 10:13). Hosea thinks of God as taking Israel back into the wilderness, there to speak tenderly with her (Hos. 2:14). When stones are quarried to be used for a building, those stones have to be hammered into shape. When we feel the hammer of God, we know

107

that we have been chosen. Should God leave us alone, life would be much easier; but it would mean that we are living to no purpose.

Apart from the specific ways in which each one of us learns what God is doing with us when we go through the experience of pain, there is also a universal truth which all must learn. Paul states this truth in what is almost a doxology. 'I am sure that neither death, nor life, nor angels, nor principalities, nor things present, nor things to come, nor powers, nor height, nor depth, nor anything else in all creation, will be able to separate us from the love of God in Christ Jesus our Lord' (Rom. 8:38–39). The love of God is enough under all circumstances. It is sufficient for every need. In purely personal terms, Paul himself bears witness to the way in which he learned the sufficiency of God's grace. 'I had a thorn in the flesh,' he says, 'given to me by Satan to harass me. I asked God over and over again to take it away, but He did not. All he said to me was—my grace is sufficient for you.'

Lastly, there is the invitation which we receive to suffer with Christ. Christ suffered because He loved even those who did not want Him to love them. This is an experience into which those who would be His disciples must enter. Only through this fellowship with His sufferings can we experience also the power of His resurrection. The experience of the cross is the experience of being at the mercy of people—at their mercy because we love them so. And then, there is the other side of the experience of the cross: that to those who have been faithful in their witness to Jesus Christ, is entrusted the gift of pain through which they can complete their witness:

Till death Thine endless mercies seal
And make the sacrifice complete.

108

Do not be afraid, keep on believing (Mark 5 : 36).

LIVING WITH GOD'S DELAYS

When Jairus comes to Jesus because his daughter is very ill, he comes expecting to take Jesus as quickly as possible to his home. But there is an unexpected delay. On the way, a woman suffering from a haemorrhage comes quietly behind the crowd and manages to touch the hem of His cloak, believing that by that touch she will be healed. Jesus stops to identify the woman. He must meet her. But, while all this is happening, time is slipping by. Jairus must somehow get Jesus to his house without further delay. And then the messengers arrive bringing the sad news to Jairus that his child is dead. It is now too late. Why trouble the Master any further? Jesus is still talking to the woman when He sees the commotion caused by the messengers who came to Jairus. He can read on the face of Jairus the message they have brought. He turns to Jairus and, ignoring what they have said, says to him, 'Do not be afraid, keep on believing.'

There is another incident in the gospels similar to this one—John 11 : 1 f. Lazarus is dying and his sisters, Mary and Martha, send word to Jesus. He is in Perea across the Jordan waiting quietly for the time when He will make His last visit to Jerusalem. His enemies are seeking to assassinate Him and He has decided to keep out of their way. He waits, therefore, for further news about His friend. When the news comes, it is too late. Lazarus is dead. Jesus immediately sets out to go to Bethany. Mary and Martha will surely expect Him. But why go when it is too late? Simply because it is never too late for Him.

When Jesus says to Jairus, 'Keep on believing', He is

saying to him, 'Was it not your faith in me that brought you to me? The situation that brought you may have changed. The God of your fathers has not changed. Was God ever too late?' Jesus raised the daughter of Jairus from the dead. Jesus raised Lazarus from the dead. Jesus still does the same, doing for us more than we think He can do. 'Eye has not seen, nor ear heard what the Lord has prepared for His children' (1 Cor. 2:9).

In the case of Jairus, not only had the situation changed, but also those who were around him, the members of his household, had lost their faith. What Jesus says to Jairus is, 'Never mind about the others, you keep on believing.'

In our life with Christ, this is a situation which can develop, that we start with our fellows on an enterprise together, and then one by one those who are with us lose heart and hope. It is at such times, when, as it were, one stands alone, that it is hard not to give way to fear, not to give way to despair. During the darkest days of the German occupation of Norway, Bishop Berggrav said, 'God is preparing a victory in the night.' He knew nothing about the preparations going on in England for the invasion of Normandy, but he knew his God. We do not always know what God has in store for us. We do not need to know. It is enough to know that whatever He has for us in His right hand are joys for evermore' (Ps. 16:11).

Lastly, the word of Jesus to Jairus was addressed to him when he himself had lost faith. 'Even when you cannot believe,' says Jesus to Jairus, 'keep on believing. Even if faith be dead, let hope be alive. Cling on to me, even though you feel that it is too late.'

Both in the stories of Jairus and the home at Bethany, the end is one of triumph. But that is not how this kind of story always ends. Time and again, the end of the story is simply that a child of God has struggled to keep his faith and his hope and has received no solution to his problem, no alleviation of misery, no intervention of God; only he was established in the experience of clinging to God whatever happens. I have often thought of Mary Magdalene standing at the foot of the cross. The man who rescued her from the past was dying. The one man who treated her with dignity was hanging there. She was alone and, as far as she knew, she was going to be alone for the rest of her life. In almost all the pictures of the crucifixion, we find two women. There is Mary, the mother of Jesus, but she is being held by John. It is Mary Magdalene who is painted alone, crouched at the feet of her dying friend. We do sometimes come to the situation in which Mary Magdalene was. It is then that we shall need grace still to stay where for us, it seems, the Saviour has died.

WEDNESDAY

Beware of practising your piety before men
(Matt. 6:1).

THE FATHER IN SECRET

In the teaching of Jesus, a very important place is given to the dangers inherent in the practice of piety. The Jewish people were pious people. It is impossible to read the story of Israel without being struck by their terrible preoccupation with God. Jesus, however, saw how the religious life could also become the self-centred life. Indeed, it was quite possible for the religious life to become the life in which it was God himself who was absent. Robert Browning paints the picture in vivid words:

As some temple seemed
My soul, where naught is changed and incense rolls
Around the altar, only God is gone
And some dark spirit sitteth in his seat.

Jesus speaks to this situation in many ways. The passage we shall think of is in the sixth chapter of Matthew's gospel in which He speaks about the practices of alms-giving, prayer and fasting.

'When you do some act of charity,' He says, 'do not let your left hand know what your right is doing, your good deed must be secret, and your Father who sees what is done in secret will reward you.' What Jesus is asking us to do is to hide our charity. We must hide it from men. Let nobody see it. It is enough for us that God sees it, for God can see what is done in secret. A life of good deeds and helpfulness can become a difficult burden to carry. There is always the desire not so much for recognition of what we have done, but for recognition of the kind of people we are. We forget that only God knows the kind of people we are; and that, therefore, there is little point in impressing other people with some particular aspect of our character of which we are proud.

In the 139th Psalm, there is real medicine for the disease which all men have, which is somehow to impress their fellow men. That God knows me is good enough to cure me of any desire that men should know me also. Should men know me as I am, life would be unsupportable. To ask that men should know me not as I am is to ask to be a hypocrite.

'O Lord, thou hast searched me and known me!
Thou knowest me when I sit down and when I rise up;
Thou discernest my thoughts from afar.
Thou searchest out my path and my lying down,
and art acquainted with all my ways.'

When speaking about prayer, Jesus says, 'Go into the room by yourself, shut the door, and pray to your Father who is there is the secret place.' About our charity, He says, 'Let your charity be a secret between your Father and yourself. Go to Him and tell Him your secret. He will like you to tell Him and you will enjoy telling Him. But you will lose His joy, if your charity is public knowledge.' Now, with regard to prayer, Jesus says, 'Remember that your Father is in the secret place.' There must be a secret place in our lives, a place where God is the secret who is kept. To parade one's prayer life is to parade one's God. Jesus seems to say, 'Let God be your secret.'

Does this mean that we may not talk about God, that we may not tell others about Him? It does and it does not. For, the point is that there is no use in talking about God to other people, if our lives do not suggest to them that God is our secret. If we do not carry about with us the scent of that secret place where we habitually dwell, then little is served by talking about it.

Concerning fasting, Jesus says, 'When you fast, anoint your head and wash your face, so that men may not see that you are fasting, but only your Father who is in the secret place; and your Father who sees what is secret will give you your reward'—*I keep it a secret. He is my secret. Only He is in the secret.*

The application of what Jesus is saying goes beyond the practices of charity, prayer and fasting. In the last analysis, the simplest way of saying it is to say that my soul is my secret in life and in death; so that the question is whether this secret is shared with God and whether only God is in the secret. Where this is not so, that empty place in the recesses of the soul does become filled with that 'dark spirit' of which the poet speaks.

THURSDAY

I fast twice a week, I give tithes of all that I get
(Luke 18 : 12).

THE BADNESS OF GOODNESS

In the teaching of Jesus which we have already con-
sidered concerning the practice of piety, there is also
implied a warning concerning the feeling of goodness
which the practice of piety may produce. It is not enough
to recognize the badness of badness. A much more in-
sidious problem is the badness of goodness. In the story of
the pharisee and the publican who went to the temple
to pray, Jesus shows us one source from which the feeling
of goodness arises. 'The pharisee prayed with himself.'
He also prayed consciously in the presence of the publican. When we compare ourselves with other people, it is
not difficult to choose such people for our comparison
as will give us a sense of superiority. The feeling that one
is good is the result not merely of remembering all the
good things that one has done, but of remembering them
away from the presence of God. No wonder this parable
was addressed to those who trusted in themselves, the
consequence of whose self-trust was that they despised
others.

The picture of the publican is of a man who did not
even trust himself to trust God. Not only did he stand
far away from the pharisee, he would not even 'lift up
his eyes to heaven'. Jesus says, 'The publican went home
justified', which is another way of saying that he went
home conscious of God's mercy to him. The pharisee had
no place for God in his scheme of things, except as a
point of reference for his own sense of righteousness.

Paul, in his letter to the Corinthians (1 Cor. 10 : 1–13),
speaks of those who felt spiritually secure because they

belonged to a community that was the community of God's people. 'Let not your sense of security be such,' he says, 'that you do not realize how insecure you are. Let anyone who thinks he stands, take heed lest he fall.' The point made is that it is possible, in the name of the community, to find ways of hiding from acceptance of individual responsibility before God, acceptance which is essential if one is to live truly. In general terms, the warning of Paul is against a feeling of goodness that is anchored in the past tense. One has to be good in the present tense. There is no point in saying, 'I have arrived', if one is slipping. There is no point in saying 'I stand', when one is about to fall. We must learn to keep our eyes fixed not on the distance we have travelled, but on the distance between us and our goal.

There is a third warning with regard to the feeling of goodness which also we must heed. When Mary broke her jar of ointment and poured it over Jesus in one act of glad abandon, Judas grumbled. Judas would have sold the ointment and put the money into a fund and with that fund organized a scheme of charity (John 12 : 3–6). There are good people who are quite incapable of imaginative acts of kindness. Their goodness has become daily routine. It has ceased to represent a living response to God. It has become just a part of the way in which they live. What was once a living response can become dead habit.

In Paul's letter to the Romans is the classic discussion of the precariousness of true goodness. Paul had lived the religious life as a Jew. He was blameless according to the law. He had then been met by the risen Christ and made Christ's own. He had lived for many years the life of a missionary, proclaiming and demonstrating the gospel. He knew what it was to live by the power of Jesus Christ and be sustained by His Grace. And yet he said to himself, 'I know that nothing good dwells within me. What dwells within me is sin' (Rom. 7 : 17–20). Goodness can never become one's own possession, it is constantly received from God through the grace of Jesus Christ; whereas sin does dwell within us in that it is an integral part of our nature. We do what we don't want to do. We don't do what we want to do. We are caught in a life of which death is the reality. In this situation, what we have to be thankful for is that this life remains open to God and that constantly from God comes the word, 'Not guilty'. To lose this sense of goodness as a gift to be received, rather than as an attainment to be won, is to lose the struggle for goodness itself.

FRIDAY

You did not choose me but I chose you and appointed you that you should go and bear fruit (John 15 : 16).

RESTORED TO FRUITFULNESS

Throughout these Lenten meditations, we have stressed again and again the previousness of the act of God in Jesus Christ. This same stress falls here also. However, it is not enough just to speak generally of the previousness of Christ's action when one is considering all that is involved in fruitful Christian living. It is necessary to think of details.

In the parable of the sower which Jesus told, some of these details are clearly mentioned (Matt. 13 : 1–9; 18–23). When the sower went out to sow, some seed fell on the road. How did there happen to be a road in the middle of the field? It is a common sight in Asian lands to see people, who want to go from one side of the field to the other, cut across the field. When for days people have done this, right across the ploughed field a path has been made. It is ploughed ground which has now become a hardened path. Jesus says, 'When the word of God fell on this path, it did not grow at all. The birds of the air picked the seed and that was the end of it.' If the ground, hardened by the constant beating of feet, was to be fruitful again, it must be ploughed again. The Christian begins with the breaking of ground by Jesus Christ. But the heart can grow hardened again. It is not improbable that the reference of the path is to the religious leaders of the time. Their religion was a settled way of life. It had to be broken up again before it could receive the seed and the seed could bear fruit.

Another lot of seed fell on rocky ground. There was good earth above the rock and so the seeds sprouted. But when tribulation or persecution came, they withered away. If rocky ground is to be made fruitful, the rocks have to be blasted. Rocky ground is good ground which has not been prepared. Before the seed is sown, it is necessary to sow dynamite. The Christian life cannot be sustained on the foundation of a superficial repentance, or traditional religion, or a conversion emotionally contrived. None of these deals with the rock. In the parable, Jesus makes the birds of the air take away the seeds that fell on the path. Fruitfulness was lost in irrelevancies, all the kinds of irrelevancies of which life is full. When Jesus speaks of the seed that fell on rocky ground, He speaks of the heat of the sun withering the plants away, heat which He compares to persecution. This heat of the sun is essential for the growth of the seed and its ripening harvest. No one can hope to bear fruit without paying the price of being a bearer of Christ's name.

Some seed fell among thorns. The ground on which the thorns grew was also good ground, but it had not been cleared. The result was that as the seed grew, the thorns also grew and choked them. In the parable, the thorns are compared to the cares of the world and the delight in riches. To be so concerned with this life that that concern produces either anxiety or avarice is to be rendered incapable of mature fruit. For a time it may be possible for the thorns and the good plants to grow side by side. But when this happens, it will not be the thorns that are ultimately choked. Long before the sowing the thorns must be cleared away. Response to the gospel has not only to be deep, it has also to be single-eyed. It is significant that whenever Jesus wanted to speak about the alternative to God, He said 'mammon'. He did not say, the devil. The quality of mammon is to become all-absorbing.

And then, there was the seed that fell on good ground and grew and brought forth fruit. Not all parts of the ground yielded fruit equally—that was inevitable. What was important was that the ground received the seed and that in it the seed was fruitful.

Here we have a story which tells us what it is that God has to do for us if we are to bear fruit and if our fruit is to remain. The path was good ground, but it had to be ploughed again. The rocky land was good ground, too, but the rocks had to be blasted. The thorns grew also on good ground, but they had to be cleared. Only God can do these things for us.

SATURDAY

You know what hour it is, how it is full time now for you to wake from sleep (Rom. 13:11).

THE TENSE OF CHRISTIAN LIFE

The Christian life is lived in the faith of a double event. The future is over; the resurrection life, the life that is beyond death, is already a present experience. But this present experience of an accomplished future is grounded in the conviction of a past which also is over. That is how the present remains exploding and explosive.

What does it mean thus to talk of the past as something which is truly past? First of all, it means that our sins are forgiven. It is characteristic of New Testament speech that forgiveness is a fact in the past tense. 'I am writing to you, my children,' says John, 'because your sins have been forgiven for His sake' (1 John 2 : 12). Paul declares, 'God was in Christ reconciling the world to himself, no longer holding men's misdeeds against them' (2 Cor. 5 : 19). The prayer of Jesus on the cross for forgiveness has been answered. Certainly, this does not mean that sinning is of no consequence, but it does mean that sin no more rules in our lives. 'The powers of evil, even though they be active, have been disarmed' (Col. 2 : 15), so that it can already be said that, 'No man who dwells in Him is a sinner' (1 John 3 :6). The exhilaration of Christian living results from this past tense in the Christian faith.

But why, if this is so, are we not as Christians and as a Christian community known by our joy? Does not the answer lie in the fact that the experience of sins forgiven has nevertheless not made us participants in the forgiving activity of God? God has forgiven us, but we refuse to forgive one another. And so we live refusing to accept the full consequence of the past tense which is ours in the gospel. We continue to live 'abiding', as John puts it, 'in death' (1 John 3 : 14).

There is another sense in which the past tense in the Christian faith affects our obedience. Let me give an example from a concern which is apposite at this time. John Wesley took the actions which finally led to the break between the people called Methodists and the

Church of England, because he was under compulsion to serve the cause of mission in the New World. There was no quarrel between John Wesley and the Church of England on any point of doctrine or order. Such quarrels arose only after the break. Today, the situation faces us in reverse. It is again the same cause of mission which is demanding that the division between these two churches should be healed. Should we be as committed to mission as John Wesley was, we would take as many risks for Union as he took when he broke with the Church of England. The past as he faced it is over; but the obedience which he rendered is still our guide as we face the present. To put it in New Testament language, the past is over because God remains the same yesterday, today, and for ever. This unchanging God is the Lord of changing history. In Him, today is the same as yesterday. That is why we are not allowed to live in our yesterdays, but are bidden to possess the truths of yesterday through contemporary obedience.

Let me give one more example, and that from Ceylon. One of the mistakes the churches made in Ceylon in the immediate past was that, as every problem arose occasioned by the social and political revolution in the midst of which they were living, they convened conferences, talked about these problems and decided to do nothing, hoping that the problems would disappear. There is an old nursery rhyme which goes like this,

> *It was last night upon the stair,*
> *I saw a man who wasn't there;*
> *He wasn't there again today,*
> *Oh, how I'd wish he'd go away.*

This is the stance of a church that does not want to move —a church satisfied with the *status quo,* a church hoping that the *status quo* can be maintained. And yet, do not our Scriptures tell us, almost on every page, that no *status quo* is secure for the Church? By its very nature it has constantly to break camp and march.

However, and here is precisely where the rub is, to keep moving is constantly to have to deal with the unknown, and many would like to escape from the unknown by withdrawing into a cloistered church. At a time when men and women are asking desperately to know God as the vis-à-vis of their daily life and living, what help can a withdrawn Christian community offer them?

God's judgement in Jesus Christ is never a judgement from afar. He comes to judge. But in this coming is involved not only His judgement, but His mercy. He who judges is also Saviour, while he who is judged is already one for whom his judge has died.

The six meditations on the meaning of forgiveness are an attempt to understand the centrality of the cross in the Christian faith and life—the way in which it gives rise to moral earnestness and saves from moral despair, the way in which it insists on life in community and also makes such life possible.

SUNDAY

And the Lord called unto Adam, and said unto him, Where art thou? (Gen. 3:9).

THE WAY BACK HOME

Adam is on his way away from home. The days of innocence are over. Paradise is left behind. He is beginning his journey to the land of the knowledge of good and evil. Henceforth he is free from God. It is in the world, in one's place of employment, in the big cities where men crowd together, in the university, that many a person finds for the first time how important his own thoughts are. He has to live by them. He determines for himself what is good and what is evil, and that which he decides to be, he finds that he has to be. There is no more anyone to protect him from himself. In Paradise, his freedom was ensured by the limited authority and power which his own decisions had. Parents, teachers, and pastors set limits to his freedom. Now there are no limits. He is at the mercy of his own will.

Soon enough he attaches himself to some group or groups. He must escape from the awful power of his aloneness and find protection in the codes of behaviour and patterns of thought of those to whom he makes himself belong. But that is only temporary respite, for God has refused to allow himself to be left behind. The sadness of that voice which said, 'Adam, where art thou?' follows him; and from that voice there is no escaping even in the university, even in one's place of employment, even in the big city. The Lamb was slain from the foundations of the world (Rev. 13:8). God accompanied man out of Paradise. Having rebelled against being bound by God's command, man has now to live in constant flight from God's pursuit. God is Emmanuel, God with us (Matt. 1:23). He is the inevitable boundary of man's life. We are either prisoners of His word or fugitives from His love.

We know that love. It never departs. It is always there wherever we are and in whatever condition. It is so utterly humble that it is willing to accept any humiliation, so utterly simple that any reason to avoid it is immediately shown to be false. 'God who is rich in mercy, has loved us in Jesus Christ' (Eph. 2:4). There is nothing more that needs to be said. 'For Christ Jesus, though he was God, counted it not something to be grasped at to cling to this glory, but emptied himself and became man and was found in the haunts of men' (Phil. 2:6–8). How empty Jesus was, so empty that no one feared to come to Him, and no one had any excuse for keeping away from Him!

The unclean leper, even from whose shadow men shrank, came to Jesus and Jesus touched him: an action which made Jesus himself unclean, so that for the stipulated period He could not enter any city (Mark 1:40-45). Children were brought to Him when He was very tired, but He received them and blessed them. The Kingdom of God belongs to children and tiredness was no reason to send them away (Mark 10:13-16). An adulteress was dragged before Him. He kept His eyes averted from her lest her shame erect a barrier between Him and her: and when she was left alone with Him, He found a way of conveying forgiveness to her (John 8:3-11). A pharisee invited Him to dinner, but refused to treat Him as an honoured guest. There was no water for His feet, nor oil for His head, nor was He given the kiss of welcome. But Jesus stayed; and at dinner that night, because of the emptiness of the Christ, God found a way of reaching Simon's soul (Luke 7:36-47). 'He emptied himself.' That is the good news of the Christian faith. Only a stable was available, but He came. How else can men meet Him except that He is willing to be among men and with men whatever the situation!

But precisely in this emptiness consists also the awkwardness of Jesus. It is because of it that we are unable to keep Him away from our lives. We satisfy ourselves by offering Him a stable, and hope that He will not come to be a permanent guest. But He comes. In our work, in our thoughts, in our plans, even in our prayers, there is only a stable for Him and yet He is there. The Church in the world, the Christian group in the business office, the fellowship of Christians in the university: these are set as common stables where the Christ will come: and, because the Christ comes, these become wherever they are an echo to men of those words spoken to Adam, 'Adam, where art thou?'

The Lamb was slain from the foundations of the world. God accompanied man out of Paradise. So that each man, whoever he is, and wherever he is, must come to terms with God. Each man takes his own road, but all men find that whatever road they take, it leads back to Him, and this time to Gethsemane. It is to Gethsemane that the road from Bethlehem leads, the road by which Jesus comes; it is also to Gethsemane that the road from Paradise leads, the road by which Judas arrives. Here in Gethsemane, God and man meet again. The intervening years have been filled with joy and sorrow, hopes aroused and hopes shattered, attempts to come to terms with Christ and attempts to force Him to come to terms with oneself, thoughts of discipleship and thoughts of disloyalty. But the final issue still remains to be settled, and it lies in that garden to which Jesus has come and where He has decided that Judas shall meet Him. 'Adam, where art thou?'—that is how the story began; 'Friend, why are you here?'—that is how the story comes to its climax.

Judas had committed himself to a cause which was the cause of his people. God would restore the Kingdom of Israel, and God's Messiah would come. So that in accepting to follow Jesus, Judas accepted Him as the answer to all his plans and all his hopes. Here was a discipleship which commanded all that he had to give. But Jesus had broken loose from the plans that Judas had made for Him; and the freedom which Judas had contrived, which was built on imprisoning God, now lay shattered because Jesus had His own way which He would take.

Jesus comes even if it be a stable we have to offer, but we cannot make Him at home there. It is our stable until He comes, but once He comes it is His territory, the spearhead of His thrust into the whole area of our lives. No wonder that we seek the only way out which is possible, which is to betray Him.

Have you been to Gethsemane? Do you know what it means to betray the Son of Man as your last desperate effort to make Him serve your ends? Do your lips tremble at the remembrance of that kiss which you gave Him when you sought to deliver Him over to His enemies in order that you might keep Him for yourself? Or is it your situation that you have not still arrived at Gethsemane, that you still find it possible to support the company of Jesus without feeling any radical opposition to Him and without encountering any radical opposition between His plans and your own?

Only those who have stood face to face with Jesus at Gethsemane know the devastating power of the words with which He greeted them : 'Friend, why are you here?' —and the overwhelming humility with which He allowed them to take Him captive. 'He emptied himself, and being found in human form he humbled himself and became obedient unto death.' How often we have seen this event take place in the lives of many whom we know! God at man's mercy because God will not leave man alone even on his journey away from Paradise—and man therefore seeking ways of rejecting God, of ejecting Him!

It is in Gethsemane that we discover that we are rebels; and that discovery we must make. Some day each one of us must see, if we have not already so seen, how brittle is our moral nature, how deceitful are our intellectual processes, and how possessive is even the very dedication by which we live. And this vision will not come until we are ourselves where Judas was, standing afar off to watch Him die whom he had betrayed.

Jesus Christ emptied himself, He became ours. He humbled himself, He put himself at our mercy. He was obedient unto death, He accepted the fate we had decreed for Him. Is it any wonder that He calls himself our servant and demands that we accept His services, if we wish to have anything to do with Him at all. It is easy to call Him Lord, it is difficult to accept Him as servant. That night when He washed the feet of the disciples, Simon Peter would not allow Him to wash his feet. Jesus said to him, 'Simon, if I do not wash you, you have no part in me' (John 13:8). You must accept the service I have come to bring. 'For the Son of Man came not to be ministered unto but to minister and give his life a ransom for many' (Mark 10:45). The Hindu finds it easy to speak of Jesus as God incarnate, but he will not accept Him as Saviour. The Buddhist is willing to speak of the Lord Jesus, but he will not accept His grace. The Muslim is willing to speak of Isa Nabi, but he will not accept His forgiveness.

Authority can take many forms. A mother's authority over her child is the authority of one who serves. So is the authority of Jesus. It took the form of a servant. We need to be broken by the humility of Jesus before we can realize who He is and what it is that He wants from us. Is Jesus your servant? Has He done for you what you could not do for yourself? Is he doing for you what you cannot do for yourself? To ask the age-old question: Are you washed in the blood of the Lamb?

Thus the journey of man proceeds: from Paradise through the dusty roads of Galilee to Gethsemane, and from Gethsemane along the Via Dolorosa to Calvary, and from Calvary—where? Judas went and bought the potter's field and hanged himself (Acts 1:18; Matt. 27:5). He could not bear any longer the love of Jesus Christ. But, oh, how wasteful that was, wasteful of his life, wasteful of his repentance, wasteful of God's forgiving grace! Judas could not forget himself even in his repentance. Even in his repentance, he had to be master of his own life. We don't truly repent until we have received that repentance itself as a gift from Him (2 Tim. 2 : 25), as part of His service to us, and so find ourselves delivered finally from being at the mercy of our own will. And then? And then, along the paths of our obedience as well as our disobedience, we meet Him, the Lord of our lives as He is the Lord of life, whose will for us has become again the acknowledged boundary of our existence, and we find Paradise again in the mastery of His fellowship.

Saul was on his way to Damascus. Jesus met him along the way (Acts 9:1–6). So to us, too, it will happen that He will meet us on every Damascus road, waylaying us along life's journey when we take the wrong turning, even sending us blindness with respect to those things which He will not have us undertake, and asking us to go to the house which He has prepared for us where it shall be told us what we must do. Within God's house, within the fellowship of the Church, there our journey ends and begins.

MONDAY

I am writing to you because your sins are forgiven for his sake (1 John 2 : 12).

THE AMBIVALENCE OF THE CHRISTIAN LIFE

The ambivalence in which the Christian life is involved is well expressed in the two sayings found in John's epistle : 'If we say we have no sin, we deceive ourselves, and the truth is not in us' (1 John 1 :8); 'No one born of God commits sin ; for God's nature abides in him, and he cannot sin because he is born of God' (1 John 3 :9). What

John is saying is that the Christian life is fundamentally a changed life. It has a new beginning in a new birth. This new beginning has to be affirmed without any qualification. And yet, within this new life with its power and its possibilities, the old life remains. To deny that this is so is to deceive oneself into a premature claim to holiness. The existence of the reality of the old life is not a denial of the reality of the new. Indeed, the reality of the new is seen in the way in which it deals with the reality of the old.

Paul explains this ambivalence, in his epistle to the Romans (Rom. 7:13-8; 8), by speaking about the ways in which sin continues to be active in his life, and yet he is delivered from condemnation through Jesus Christ in whom he now lives. The demand the Christian has to meet is the demand to have faith in Jesus Christ—to respond to His love, to be loyal in His service, to trust Him for everything. He who is in Christ has been delivered from the demand of the law which is that he be righteous.

The inner integrity of this kind of life and the only way in which this ambivalence can be sustained is to enter, in all its seriousness, into the experience of forgiveness which lies at the heart of all Christian living. Why is this so? Because the experience of forgiveness in the Christian life is not simply an experience of how the guilt of wrongdoing is dealt with. It is rather an experience by which the true relationship between God and man is renewed and established, a relationship which concerns man's interior life and its experience of God's mercy, as well as man's life in the world and his participation in God's purposes.

As one looks at the nature of the religious life as it is set forth in the various religious traditions, one sees that the religious life is primarily understood in one of three ways. First, there is the fact of man's needs in the process of daily living. It is for the securing of the wherewithal to meet these needs that the practices of prayer and penance, magic and merit are intended. Secondly, there is the mystery of life in its manifoldness and its unity which the human spirit is constantly seeking to probe. The practices that lead to ecstatic experiences as well as the practices which lead to inner withdrawal are an attempt to probe this mystery. Thirdly, there is man's involvement in wrongdoing and his search for deliverance from the sense of guilt and for the restoration of his fellowship with God. The ways of *bakthi* and devotion, confession and repentance, taught in the various religions are all intended towards this end.

But, while these three aspects of the religious life are true for the Christian faith also, they are subordinate to a deeper and wider concern. The thrust of the Christian message is not primarily about life and its needs, or life and its mystery, or life and its involvement in sin, but about life and its destiny. Its message is about a new creation, a new humanity and, therefore, about the pilgrimage and adventure of life looking forward to a great consummation and a final fulfilment. To live the forgiven life is to participate in this life. It is to become those who know what it means to be forgiven and what it means to participate in the forgiving activity of God. His forgiving activity is the source of the new creation and the hope of its fulfilment.

Speak tenderly to Jerusalem, and cry to her that her warfare is ended, that her iniquity is pardoned, that she has received from the Lord's hand double for all her sins (Is. 40:2).

THE REMISSION OF PUNISHMENT

It is said of Dr William Miller, the great Principal of Madras Christian College, that one of his students was reported to him for some serious offence. He spoke to the student gravely about his offence until the student saw the meaning of what he had done, accepted it and asked his Principal's forgiveness. Dr Miller then said to the young man, 'Son, I forgive you. Now come for the punishment.' He then took him to the office to administer the punishment. The question is, was the student forgiven? Dr Miller's action implies the answer that forgiveness is not identical with the remission of punishment.

In the letter to the Hebrews we read, 'Which son is there whom his father chasteneth not? If indeed you are not chastened, then are you bastards and not sons' (Heb. 12:8). Dr Miller may have had to punish the student because it was necessary to make the whole college understand that the behaviour for which the student was punished was wrong and would never be tolerated. The student may have been punished because his Principal felt that he was the kind of person who needed punishment to buttress his own decision not to repeat the same fault again. Or the punishment may have been thought to be necessary to prevent people thinking that a glib repentance was a way out of the consequences of serious misdemeanour. In any case, the point is that whether punishment is to be meted out or not or what kind of punishment is to be meted out, the actual punishment be decided on its own merits. That the fault has been forgiven is a separate transaction.

The question can be asked—does God punish? Or are we merely talking about the natural consequences of sin? If a person should become an alcoholic, he will pay in his body the consequences of his wrongdoing even after he has repented and reformed and been forgiven. Does this kind of example illustrate what we mean when we talk about God's punishment? I do not think so. The writer to the Hebrews surely means more than that when he speaks of God as chastening His sons. In the Old Testament story, the exile of Israel in Babylon is described as punishment. This is certainly more than consequence.

The connection between consequence and punishment may be explained thus. A child goes out in the hot sun to play and comes home with a sick headache. The mother says to him, 'I have told you over and over again not to go out in the hot sun, and that if you do, you will fall ill. So never do it again. Also, as a punishment for going out in the hot sun this time, you will not get your share of the pudding at dinner tonight.' The mother's decision to add punishment to consequence is a decision made on the basis of her understanding of her child. In fact, the punishment shows that the mother is accepting her obligation as mother, responsible for her child. Looked at in this way, the punishment meted out is itself a sign of the forgiven relationship in which the child and mother stand.

*Do good to those who hate you, bless those who
curse you, pray for those who abuse you*
(Luke 6:27–28).

GOOD FOR EVIL

What then is forgiveness, if it is not the remission of
punishment? In the story of Joseph and his brethren we
have a very good example of another common misunderstanding of the nature of forgiveness. There is very little
doubt of the fact that Joseph as a younger brother be-
haved himself in such a way as to prove offensive to his
older brothers. He was, besides being his father's favourite
son, also a prig and a boaster. Finally, his brothers could
not stand him any longer and got rid of him by selling
him to some Midianite tradesmen. The story develops
in such a way that later these same brothers had to
come to Joseph seeking his help. When finally Joseph
reveals himself to them, it is in a situation where they are
at his mercy. They expect him to punish them for what
they had done to him. But he forgives them and, as a
token of his forgiveness, sends for his father and settles
them all in a very fertile part of the land of Goshen.
After many years, during which Jacob and his sons have
enjoyed the kindness of Joseph, Jacob dies. Joseph and
his brothers go to Canaan to bury their father.

Let us read what the record says at this point (Gen.
50:14): 'After he had buried his father, Joseph returned
to Egypt with his brothers and all who had gone up with
him to bury his father. When Joseph's brothers saw that
their father was dead, they said, It may be that Joseph
will hate us and pay us back for all the evil which we did
to him. So they sent a message to Joseph, saying, Your

father gave this command before he died, Say to Joseph, Forgive I pray you, the transgression of your brothers and their sin, because they did evil to you. And now, we pray you, forgive the transgression of the servants of the God of your father.' It is said that Joseph wept when they spoke to him thus.

In spite of the fact that Joseph's brothers enjoyed kindness at his hands, they did not feel forgiven. For years Joseph had looked after them, but somehow not only had the sense of guilt remained with them, but also fear that one day Joseph would pay them back. Why was this so?

Doing good for evil need not in itself be a token of forgiveness. It is quite possible to do good to those who have wronged us without forgiving them. One is almost tempted to say that in the injunction of Paul, 'If your enemy is hungry, feed him; if he is thirsty, give him drink; for by so doing, you will heap burning coals upon his head' (Rom. 12:20), the good done is itself intended to be a way of paying back. Of course, Paul guards himself against this interpretation by adding, 'Do not be overcome by evil, but overcome evil with good.' The point, however, is that very rarely can an evil-doer be reformed by showering good upon him. When Jesus speaks of God as making His sun shine on the good and evil alike and making His rain to fall on the just and unjust, He is intending to emphasize the way in which a person must always act out of his own nature rather than in response to what somebody else has done to him. When he acts in response to the action of another, he is allowing that other action to determine what he does. We must never allow somebody else's character to decide what we shall do. And, if evil finds lodgement in our character, the way to overcome it is by letting our own character assert itself in the doing of good.

What then of the problem of forgiveness itself, if the doing of good for evil cannot mediate the sense of being forgiven?

I will not execute my fierce anger, for I am God and not man (Hos. 11 :9).

EARNING THE RIGHT TO FORGIVE

So we ask again, what is forgiveness? In the story of Hosea and Gomer, we get much closer to the real meaning of forgiveness than in any other story in the Old Testament. The central fact of the story is that Hosea loved Gomer and that there was nothing which Gomer could do or did that destroyed that love. In the way in which Hosea tells the story, it is not clear whether Gomer had already a reputation when Hosea married her. It looks probable. Hosea reports what God said to him in the words, 'Go, take to yourself a wife of harlotry.'

In spite of Hosea's love for her, a love that found her in spite of her reputation, Gomer proved unfaithful. Hosea describes the many ways by which he sought to win her back to faithfulness and to love. He pleaded with her. He got her children to plead with her. He restricted her movements, building, as he says, a hedge around her. He deprived her of opportunities to meet her lovers. He gave her everything she wanted. He took away everything she had. He allured her into the wilderness and spoke tenderly to her. But it was all of no avail. Gomer's final act was to leave Hosea permanently and sell herself away to another man. But even then Hosea did not forsake her. Poor as he was, he gave the proceeds of a whole barley harvest to buy her back.

The story is incomplete; for Hosea does not tell us whether he finally succeeded with his wife. But, whether he succeeded or not, the whole thrust of Hosea's story is to demonstrate what forgiveness really means and really costs. One may, as it were, imagine a moment when Gomer finally said to Hosea, 'Forgive me, I shall never go off again.' Hosea had forgiveness to give because he had been forgiving always. He loved her so much and so resolutely that even though the behaviour of Gomer hurt him and wounded him, he went on loving. He had earned the right to forgive.

Too often we speak one-sidedly of those who have done wrong earning the right to be forgiven. Certainly, they must. There can be no reconciliation and restoration of fellowship where forgiveness is not appropriated by repentance and confession, and made the basis of a new beginning in true amendment of life. But what is often forgotten is that not only must the wrongdoer earn the right to be forgiven, he who has been wronged has to earn the right to forgive. When someone wrongs me, if I should say to him and to myself, 'That is the end of our relationship, I will have nothing more to do with you', then, even if that person should repent, he would come to me in vain for forgiveness. I would have no forgiveness to give him. I can say, 'I forgive you' and mean by that that 'I will not harm you in return for what you have done to me.' I can even say, 'I forgive you', and mean by that that 'I am prepared to be good to you, even though you were bad to me.' But I cannot say, 'I forgive you', and mean by that that 'I give you my love.' Love has to be a permanent attitude which is prepared to suffer if need be at the hands of the person loved. Where such love is absent, it is futile to talk of forgiveness.

In the story of Joseph and his brethren, they never had proof that Joseph really loved them, and that he had suffered in spirit as the result of what they had done to him. The result was that Joseph failed to convey to them a real sense of being forgiven. Forgiveness has to be wrought with tears.

But there is forgiveness with thee, that thou mayest be feared (Ps. 130 : 4).

THE PRICE OF FORGIVENESS

At the heart of the Christian message is the story of the cross. God has earned the right to forgive. But the story of the cross says to us even more than that, in that the price which God paid to forgive reveals also the true dimension of human sin. The message of the cross is that the whole price of sin has been paid. God has accepted to bear in Jesus Christ all that sin can do and all that sin is.

First of all, there are the acts of sin which need to be forgiven—the deeds of disobedience and rebellion, unfaithfulness and disloyalty. The burden of these sinful actions is that they were actions against God. It is in their reference to Him that we see them in their true dimension. Suppose I spread a scandal against someone. Such an action is, in the last analysis, an action against God. I have betrayed my own nature as the child of God. I have also stolen his good name from someone who is my brother and for whom, therefore, God holds me responsible. To spread a scandal can seem a trivial thing until it is seen as an action against God. The whole gospel story shows us how it was sins like this, all kinds of pettiness and anger and hypocrisy and fear and self-interest, which finally crucified Jesus. When we say that by the cross the price of sin is paid, we mean that God cared so intensely for men, both in their relation to Him and to one another that He allowed the sins which they did to become His concern. He allowed them to become sins against himself. 'I have sinned against heaven' was the confession of the prodigal (Luke 15 : 21). Indeed, it is possible for me so not to care, so that what other people do against me, does not really touch me or hurt me. If I should insulate or isolate myself in this way, I can prevent myself getting hurt, but I am unable to forgive.

Secondly, there is the sinner to be forgiven, for forgiveness is not a transaction that concerns deeds only. It is a transaction between persons. In a court of law, the question to be decided is—did he do this? The kind of person he is may have something to do with the nature of the punishment meted out; but, basically, the question asked is about the deeds. The basic question which God asks from man, however, is not about his deeds but about himself. When I stand before the cross, I do not simply confess my sins, I confess myself a sinner. When we say that Jesus paid the price of sin, we mean that He so identified himself with us that what our sins do to us, they did to Him also. He did not die instead of me. He died because He became myself. When I look at Him, I see what it means to be a sinner—to be someone whose fellowship with God is broken. It was my cry which He cried when He said, 'My God, my God, why have you forsaken me?'

But, there is a third dimension to the word sin. Sin denotes, not only sins, not only sinners, but also sinfulness. Sins are never purely individual actions, they are the consequences of the state of sinfulness in which all humanity is. To confess one's sins is to go even beyond confessing oneself a sinner. It is to take one's place with one's fellowmen and to say without qualification, 'We

138

have erred and strayed from Thy ways like lost sheep. We have followed too much the devices and desires of our own hearts. We have offended against Thy holy laws. We have left undone those things which we ought to have done; And we have done those things which we ought not to have done; And there is no health in us.'

When Paul speaks of Jesus as having been made sin on our behalf (2 Cor. 5:21), this is essentially what he is talking about—that Jesus became the place where sin wrought its work. He was humanity, and sin so wrought its work on Him that it, too, became manifest, stripped of all its disguises and, therefore, identified and identifiable (Col. 2:15). The strength of sin lies in its incognito. When it is exposed, it wilts. Jesus exposed it in His own person.

SATURDAY

He who has the Son has life; he who has not the Son has not life (1 John 5:12).

AN INDIVISIBLE INHERITANCE

If this then be the logic of the cross, it becomes understandable how that the teaching of the New Testament on forgiveness is firmly anchored in Christ's ministry of reconciliation. When we say that God forgives, we mean finally that God has forgiven, that the whole of humanity is sustained by that forgiveness and that, through the ministry of the Holy Spirit, there is being achieved a reconciliation between man and God. The experience of forgiveness in its fullest Christian sense goes beyond the experience of being forgiven into the experience of sharing in the forgiving activity of God.

We can see how this applies directly to our relationships with one another. Should someone wrong me, to the extent that it was wrong, his action would be an action against God. The cry, 'Against Thee only have I sinned' (Ps. 51:4), is not just an exaggeration caused by a mood of repentance. It is against God that men sin, even when they sin against one another. But God forgives the man who has sinned against me, so that when I refuse to forgive him, what I am doing is really to say that God should not forgive him. Sometimes people say, 'Even if I forgive you, God won't forgive you.' That is pure nonsense. The fact is that by refusing to participate in God's act of forgiveness I stand outside His act, an act which includes me as well as everyone else. There is only one forgiveness, and no man can expect to enjoy his own little bit all by himself. The experience of God's forgiveness is for men an indivisible and undivided heritage. In His parable of the two sons, Jesus has shown us plainly how the elder brother puts himself outside the fellowship of the home because he will not share in his father's forgiveness of the younger brother.

There is another way also of looking at this, and that is to recognize that when God forgives me, He does it in such a way that His love overflows my life. I cannot so restrict God's love for me that I contain it within my own interests and my own needs. It will overflow. And on that overflowing depends also my experience of it. When Scripture says, 'Freely you have received, freely give' (Matt. 10:8), it is teaching us the only way in which we can receive. To receive is to be able to give and to give is to be able to receive.

Now we can get back to the point at which we began this study on forgiveness and see how, in this experience of the forgiven life, is held both the working out of the new life which is the consequence of the new birth, and the dismantling of the old life which remains active in spite of the fact that it is passing away. For the ambivalence of the new and the old never results in a situation in which forgiveness becomes less and less necessary. Rather, the situation is increasingly one in which forgiveness is felt to be a necessity because one sees not only the badness of badness but the badness of goodness as well.

No wonder, then, that in the Christian faith, the community of heaven is described not as an aristocracy of the good but as the fellowship of the forgiven.

THE END OF LENT

It is a long road by which we have come in our meditations this lenten season. We have seen what it means to be summoned to faith as well as what it means to maintain that faith in the journey of life. Now we come to the end of this period of Lent, remembering that this season only provides us with the opportunity for a review, a review that is intended to strengthen resolve and deepen dedication, so that when life's journey is actually over, it may be said of each one—'He kept the faith.'

EASTER SUNDAY

I intend always to remind you of these things
(2 Peter 1 : 12).

THE CALL TO REMEMBER

Easter Sunday is a good time to say: 'Ebenezer'—'Hitherto the Lord has helped us' (1 Sam. 7 : 12). He has brought us to this hour and to this place. We remember and are thankful. Over and over again this exhortation to remember comes in Holy Scripture—comes at moments of crisis when hope must be held fast, comes during periods of transition when purpose must remain sure, comes as plans are overturned when obedience must remain resolute, comes in hours of achievement when faith must scan the road that still has to be travelled.

The text for this Easter meditation occurs in a passage in which the writer speaks of his impending death. He wants to ensure that those to whom he is writing will always hold certain things in remembrance. 'I intend', he says, 'always to remind you of these things, that after my departure, you may be able at any time to recall them.' 'For', he continues, 'this to which I call you to pay attention, will be for you as a lamp shining in a dark place, until the day dawns and the morning star rises in your hearts.'

This figure of a lamp shining in a dark place was a figure used by our Lord. According to Him, we who bear His name are the light of the world—not the light of the morning when the day has dawned, but the light of a little lamp burning in a dark place. There is just sufficient light with which men can see, just sufficient light in which they can walk. However, it is night. In this Second Letter of Peter, this same figure of a little lamp shining in a dark place is used to refer to those convictions and memories by which the soul is kept alight in the midst of its doubts and uncertainties, even in the midst of its sin and rebellion. The truth concerning ourselves, as lamps shining in a dark place, is necessarily dependent on this second truth. We are not ourselves the light. Should we be able to shed light, it is because there is a light in us: the light that was lit by what God wrought in us and for us, and which is fed by the conscious remembrance of this which God has wrought and all that it portends.

It will not be wrong to say that, in the case of many, their faith has grown dim and their hopes have gone sour and their enthusiasms have gone cold, simply because memory has not been allowed to hold the door. There are no remembered yesterdays—whether they be the yesterdays when things happened or when things were promised, whether they be the yesterdays of achievement or vocation. What then are the memories to which we are bidden? Our text strikes a directly personal note. It calls us to remember what belongs intimately to our own stories and the stories of those who have gone before us and into whose labours we have entered.

Of the remembrances to which we are bidden, the first that we shall consider is told us in a word from the prophet of the exile. *Hearken to me, you who pursue deliverance, You who seek the Lord; Look to the rock from which you were hewn, And to the quarry from which you were digged* (Is. 51:1).

Here is a call to remember from where we have come. As I face this call, my mind goes back to my father's grandfather, who was a Hindu lad growing up in a poor home in a little village in Ceylon. Anxious to get an education and entrust himself to somone who would look after him, he walked to the nearest mission station and gave himself to the missionary who was there. On the day of his baptism a few years later he gave his witness in these words: 'I went looking for shelter and found a shell and in that shell I found a pearl.' My mind also goes back to my mother's great-grandmother, who was the eldest of six daughters. A missionary, going for a walk through the village, came one day upon a little scene —a mother and her seven daughters sitting round a pot of gruel. They were obviously poor. The missionary said to the mother, 'Would you like me to take your eldest daughter and look after her?' The mother consented. The girl had no choice. As the girl followed the missionary, she prayed to her god to deliver her from the hands of this foreigner. So the story begins concerning the rock from which I was hewn and the quarry from which I was digged.

All who have shared in these meditations will have similar memories, of how God's long arm reached out and found, not only their forefathers, but also found them. And, as our memories reach back, our minds become alert in remembrance of all those who are today still where our forebears were; still part of that rock, still part of that quarry. Does not such remembrance put a resolve into our souls and a task into our hands, that they who do not know, shall know?

But, and here I think I speak for all in the household of faith, each one will find that to remember what God has wrought for him is not enough. We are such insignificant people that, in order to confirm our faith, we shall have again and again to call the roll of honour in our minds. The writer of the epistle to the Hebrews calls that roll. It gave him and his readers courage to know themselves as part of all that company. There is a poignant psalm in which the psalmist says, 'From the ends of the earth I call to thee, when my heart is faint.' And then speaking of the way in which God has answered his cry he says, 'Thou, O God, hast heard my vows, Thou hast given me the heritage of those who fear Thy name' (Ps. 61 : 1–5).

When my wife and I were at the World Council of Churches Assembly at Evanston, my wife bought a Bible and got many of those who were there to sign on its cover page. When I asked her what she intended to do with it, she said, 'This Bible is for my son. Whenever he feels depressed or doubting, he can read these names and say to himself—the God of Visser 'tHooft and Franklin Fry and Martin Niemoller and Pierre Maury and John Baillie and Josef Hromadka is my God.' Lately, I was talking to a lady who was in great distress. She was a person who in recent months had drifted away from the fellowship of the Church. I said to her, 'Sometimes God does seem distant; but it is at such times that we must cling to our fellow believers. You find yourself helpless, because you thought you could cling to God alone.'

To remember the rock from which we were hewn, and the quarry from which we were dug, is also to remember one another.

Scripture calls us not only to remember from where we have come, but also to remember from what we were brought. Central to the Ten Commandments, which Moses gave to the people, was this bidding: *You shall remember that you were a servant in the land of Egypt, and the Lord your God brought you out thence, with a mighty and outstretched arm* (Deut. 5:15). There is a slavery from which we were rescued. We were not merely powerless ourselves, but no one who was a man could have rescued us. The exhortations of morality, the wisdom of philosophy, the disciplines of mysticism, even the practices of religion, were powerless to set us free. God stretched out His arm in mercy and found us. God became our God in Jesus Christ.

But, and here lies the crux of the matter, this memory of a captivity from which we were delivered is what must feed our determination to accept with gladness the captivity into which we have been brought.

'I delivered you, therefore you must keep my commandments.'

'I gave you rest, therefore you must accept my yoke.'

'I was your succour, when you were a stranger and an alien, therefore you must brother all those who are strangers in your midst—the homeless, the stateless, the refugee.'

We shall never be so set free that we can be our own

masters. We must either be captive to power or be captive to love. We shall have either to undertake the tasks that power sets us, or the tasks to which love beckons. The cry for freedom will always be wedded to the responsibility for new tasks.

Strangely enough, however, when referring to Egypt, Scripture bids Israel not only to remember but also to forget. '*Thus says the Lord, I will put an end to your lewdness and your harlotry brought out from the land of Egypt; so that you shall not lift up your eyes to the Egyptians or remember them anymore*' (Ezek. 23:27). Israel never quite lost its yearning for the fleshpots of Egypt. The worship of the golden calf which they had learned in Egypt continued to fascinate them, and all the practices associated with that worship were a perennial temptation. It is true that we have been delivered, but the past is still with us, and demands from us constant striving and eternal vigilance. Indeed, it demands more than that. For we have not understood the seriousness of our situation until we have cried, 'Oh, wretched man that I am'; and until we have shouted, 'Thank God through Jesus Christ.'

The two remembrances which we have spoken about coalesce in a third. When we remember from where we have come and from what we were brought, we remember also to whom we belong now. At the heart of the Church's faith and worship is an act of remembrance. *The Lord Jesus, on the night when he was betrayed, took bread and when he had given thanks, he broke it, and said, This is my body which is broken for you. Do this in remembrance of me* (1 Cor. 11:23–24). This act of remembrance, by which the Church lives and through which it worships, has a double thrust. First of all, it is our constant reminder that we are not our own. We live

147

because someone has died; so that we who live belong to Him. And secondly, because He who died has died for all, we are not our own also in a further sense. We belong to them. 'As often as you eat this bread and drink this cup,' says Paul, 'you proclaim the Lord's death until he comes' (1 Cor. 11:26). This proclamation that Paul is talking about is not a proclamation simply in word and sacrament. It is a proclamation in life. In the earlier English translation, the word used is 'shew forth'. People must be able to look at us and see in us His death at work. 'While we live,' says Paul, writing to the Corinthians, 'we are always being given up to death for Jesus' sake . . . So death is at work in us but life in you (2 Cor. 4:12).

Let me attempt a simple illustration to get at what is meant here. A Christian leader in China, writing to a friend abroad, says, 'Do not pray at us, do not even pray for us, but pray with us.' How much dying we shall have to do before we can answer this appeal of our Chinese brethren! The practice of death is the only way to enter into the ministry of the incarnation. Christ's death is a death into which we must die continually.

But the commonest call to remembrance in Scripture, is the call to remember the Lord's mercies. *Bless the Lord, O my soul: and all that is within me, bless His holy name. Bless the Lord, O my soul, and forget not all His benefits* (Ps. 103:1–2). He has brought us to this day and to this hour. His patience with us has been unwearied, and His love for us has remained steadfast. He has led us by paths we did not anticipate and given us blessings for which we never asked.

And yet how difficult we find it to remember His mercies to us. In one of the meditations of Dr Kagawa, there is a very telling comment on this experience. He says, 'The trouble with most Christians is that they do not know how to count. A child learns to count 1, 2, 3, 4; but most of us count 100, 99, 98, 97. Instead of counting what we have, we count what we don't have.' How true it is! If I had everything I wanted, it would be 100. I do not have a car, and therefore it is 99. I do not like my job and therefore it is 96. I am not very happy with my wife or husband and therefore it is 85. A well-known gospel song puts the matter simply and directly:

> *Count your blessings, name them one by one,*
> *And it will surprise you what the Lord has done.*

Let no one think that here we are talking about a psychological device, a device to keep the mind contented and satisfied. The point is that we must remember that what we have been given defines the situation within which we have to render our thanks and offer our obedience. They spell for us where we are. We cannot meet God except at the place where life's circumstances have placed us. Often the problem, however, is that, whereas God is willing to begin with us where we are, we ourselves are not willing. We want to begin from somewhere else. God calls a young man to serve His Church in the ordained ministry, but the young man is anxious lest people say that he joined the ministry because he could not make good in any other career. Or, God wants someone to teach in the Sunday school, but this someone would rather wait to serve God until she gets married to a rich man and is able to give large donations to the Church. Or, God opens the way for a person to witness to Him in public life, but this person would rather wait till Sunday comes, when he can preach in safety at the Sunday morning service. So the instances can be multiplied.

There is a song which runs:

> *Three o'clock on Sunday afternoon—*
> *All the week to wait for it!*
> *Wash and wipe each plate for it!*
> *Frightened I'll be late for it!*
> *Three o'clock! he'll turn that corner soon!—*

A girl is to meet her boy by the pillar-box in the corner of Berkeley Square at three in the afternoon. She is singing as she takes her place. After each verse, the clock chimes another quarter, but there is still no young man. At the end of the hour, she has given up and is marching off, pretending that she does not care, when a passing policeman asks her if she is waiting for anybody, because, he says, 'There's a young man by a pillar-box at the corner of Grosvenor Square'—

> *Here's a change of air for you,*
> *A walk to Grosvenor Square for you;*
> *You'll find him waiting there for you—*
> *At four o'clock on Sunday afternoon!*

How many are waiting for God in vain, because they are waiting at the wrong pillar-box!

And lastly, there is the bidding of Scripture that we remember to keep looking for the dawn. It is when dawn comes and the morning star has appeared that our task too will be over. Then all lamps become unnecessary. There is no necessity even for the sun or the moon; for the glory of God is the light of the City of Salvation and its lamp is the Lamb (Rev. 21:23).

In Peter's first letter, the way he is writing suggests the picture of a besieged city. The conditions within the city are difficult. 'But', he says, 'do not yield, do not surrender, do not raise the white flag. Set your hope fully upon the grace that is coming to you at the revelation of Jesus Christ' (1 Pet. 1:13). Succour is already on the way, victory has already been prepared. In one of the unforgettable passages in Isaiah, there is a cry: *Watchman, what of the night? The Watchman answers, Morning comes, and also the night. If you will inquire, inquire; Come back again* (Is. 21:11–12). Cannot we hear this answer of the watchman in all our lands today? 'The morning comes and also the night.'

There is more of the night to come. The problems and difficulties, heartaches and tragedies of our human living together will not be solved tomorrow or the day after. Many hours of the night must still be lived through, and some of these hours will seem to go on leaden feet. But the watchman's answer was, 'The morning comes, and also the night.' The night is the night before the dawn. Midnight has struck already. It was midnight when Jesus died on Calvary. So that time is now set towards the morning. For this morning, we must wait, and we must work. It is sure.

The watchman also adds to his answer, 'If you want to inquire again, come again.' We shall indeed want to inquire again. Hope will dim and faith will falter. We shall work and find that we have nothing to show for our working. We shall think and discover that we are simply thinking in circles. It will look again and again as if the night is deepening. And yet when we inquire again, it will be the same answer that we shall receive, 'He is risen and goes befor you into Galilee' (Mark 16:6–7).